Dramasc

Love and Loss

Lady of Flowers and Feathers

Dead Man

Queen of Hearts

Three traditional tales dramatised by

DAVID CALCUTT

with explanatory notes and activities

Nelson

Nelson
Nelson House
Mayfield Road
Walton-on-Thames
Surrey KT12 5PL
United Kingdom

Project management by Elizabeth Paren
Designed and formatted by Geoffrey Wadsley
Art editing by Jane Taylor
Edited by Alison Hart
Cover illustration by Dave Grimwood, Pelican Graphics
Black and white illustrations by Pat Moffett (*Lady of Flowers and Feathers* and *Queen of Hearts*) and Judy Stevens (*Dead Man*)
Printed by L. Rex Printing Co. Ltd, China

This edition first published by Nelson 2000
ISBN 0-17-432615-7
9 8 7 6 5 4 3 2 1
03   02   01   00

Acknowledgements
The author and publisher are grateful for permission to include the following copyright material: extract from *Math, Son of Mathonwy*, from J.M. Dent and Son Everyman's Library, translated by Gwyn Jones and Thomas Jones, first published 1949 and revised in 1974, Orion Publishing, London; and extract from Euripides 'Alcestis', Lattimore, trans., in Lattimore *The Greek Tragedies*, *vol 3*, published by the University of Chicago Press.

Every effort has been made to trace all the copyright holders, but where this has not been possible the publisher will be pleased to make any necessary arrangements at the first opportunity.

CONTENTS

SERIES EDITOR'S INTRODUCTION

Dramascripts is an exciting series of plays especially chosen for students in the lower and middle years of secondary school. The titles range from the best in modern writing to adaptations of classic texts such as *A Christmas Carol* and *Silas Marner*.

Dramascripts can be read or acted purely for the enjoyment and stimulation that they provide; however, each play in the series also offers all the support that pupils need in working with the text in the classroom:

- **Introduction** – this offers important background information and explains something about the ways in which the play came to be written.
- **Script** – this is clearly set out in ways that make the play easy to handle in the classroom.
- **Notes** explain references that pupils might not understand, and language points that are not obvious.
- **Activities** – at the end of scenes, acts or sections – give pupils the opportunity to explore the play more fully. Types of activity include: discussion, writing, hot-seating, improvisation, acting, freeze-framing, story-boarding and artwork.
- **Looking Back at the Play** – this section has further activities for more extended work on the play as a whole, with emphasis on characters, plots, themes and language.

John O'Connor

WORLDWIDE DRAMASCRIPTS

Whether we look at the Caribbean or China, ancient India or medieval Europe, we find that cultures across the world and throughout history have had one fundamental thing in common: they have all created myths, legends and traditional tales, in an endeavour to make sense of their existence and to confront the most challenging issues of right and wrong.

Worldwide Dramascripts present some of the most exciting and intriguing examples of these tales in the form of lively and thought-provoking playscripts. These bring together figures such as Theseus and Rama, Anansi and Guinevere, Hanuman the monkey-god and the famous Lambton Worm.

With the exception of *Goat Song* – an original retelling of Greek myths in a single play – each anthology brings together three or four short plays with a connecting theme, raising questions about:

- right and wrong
- justice and retribution
- the nature of heroism
- the eternal tensions between brothers and sisters
- the joys and pain of love
- the never-ending need to escape.

Because they feature such basic human concerns the plays and activities in Worldwide Dramascripts offer opportunities for students to engage with issues of enduring significance while enjoying some of the greatest stories ever told.

John O'Connor

INTRODUCTION

The three plays in this collection are based on stories from three cultures – Celtic, Ancient Greek, and Indian. Although, on the face of it, the three cultures and the societies those cultures sprang from are very different, they are, in fact, much more closely related than we might think. And the reason we know they are closely related has to do with language. Just over two hundred years ago an Englishman named Sir William Jones, who was serving as a judge in India, undertook a close study of the ancient Indian language of Sanskrit. Although most of the earliest Indian texts were written in Sanskrit, it had not been used as a spoken language for many hundreds of years, like ancient Greek and Latin. In 1786, Jones discovered that the way Sanskrit was structured was remarkably similar to the way in which ancient Greek and Latin were structured. He realised, in fact, that Sanskrit, ancient Greek, and Latin were related. And he went on to discover that most of the languages of Europe – the German and Celtic languages, the languages of Eastern Europe and of the Middle East – were also related in the same way. And this means that all these languages must have sprung from the same source – some unknown language spoken by an unknown people far back in time. This unknown people, in other words, were the common ancestors of many of the peoples in Europe, the Middle East and India – all those great and diverse cultures and civilisations had their beginnings in the same place with the same people, who spoke the same language – and shared the same stories.

Given this, it seems more or less certain that the myths of Ancient Greece, India, Rome, the Middle East, Celtic Europe, and all the rest, also sprang from a common stock of stories. Further than that, it seems to me that the three stories in this book can perhaps be seen, not just as separate tales, but as three episodes from the same tale. In choosing to dramatise them, and in placing them in the order in which they appear, this is what I had in mind. Although the names of the characters may change from play to play, and although the settings may change from Britain to Greece and to India, they are, in essence, a single drama. And the story this drama tells is of human attempts to overcome the natural forces of the world – forces which they feel hold them in chains, and which, if they do not overcome them, will destroy them. In other words, it tells the ancient story of humanity's struggle to overcome Death.

Seeing the plays as episodes in a single drama led me to adopt a similar style of writing for them – a simple, plain, pared-down style, with an emphasis on the use of narrative and storytelling. I see them too as being performed like this.

David Calcutt

Dramascripts

Lady of Flowers and Feathers

Dramatised by

DAVID CALCUTT

BACKGROUND TO THE PLAY

The play is based on part of a Welsh story called *Math, Son of Mathonwy*. This story is one of four, known collectively as *The Four Branches of the Mabinogion*. They were written down, in Welsh, in the fourteenth century, and are generally regarded as masterpieces of medieval literature. But the material they deal with, the characters and incidents that make up the stories, are much older, going back to pre-Christian times. In other words, the stories are memories of ancient myths, and the characters based on pagan Celtic gods, goddesses and heroes. What these original myths and tales were is difficult to work out. The Celts had been living in Britain for several hundred years by the time the Romans came here, and were a highly civilised people – but they had no common system of writing. Their myths – which are a record of a people's religion – were passed by word of mouth, using a highly developed memory system, so that nothing was lost or forgotten. But when the Romans came here they outlawed the Celtic religion, destroyed its sacred places, suppressed its practice. The myths, like many of the people themselves, went into hiding in the remote areas of the country – especially Wales. There, they were cherished by the survivors of the Roman conquest, and continued to be passed on by word of mouth from generation to generation. But that highly developed memory system had broken down and, over the following centuries, the myths changed with each telling, new material and influences were added to them, elements were forgotten or confused. And, by the time they were written down, the land had been Christian for several hundred years, and the myths had been filtered through this new religious system and world-view. Yet, when you read the stories – which are beautiful examples of medieval literature – it is still possible to sense the mystery and majesty of those original myths, lying there at the heart, the source of energy and vitality, not dead, but living still.

THE CHARACTERS

(in order of appearance)

CERRIDWEN *a pig.*

GWYDION *a wizard.*

MATH *King of Gwynedd.*

LLEW *Math's son.*

ARIANHROD *Llew's mother.*

BLODEUWEDD *Llew's wife, a woman made from flowers.*

GRONW *Blodeuwedd's lover, Lord of Penllyn.*

PRONOUNCING THE NAMES

CERRIDWEN *Cer-rid-when*

GWYDION *Goo-eed-ee-on*

MATH *Maa-th*

LLEW *Ll-eh-oo (For ll sound, put tongue in 'l' position and try to hiss.)*

ARIANHROD *Ar-ee-an-rod*

BLODEUWEDD *Blor-they-weh-th*

GRONW *Gronn-oo*

LADY OF FLOWERS AND FEATHERS

T*he stage is simply an empty space, which represents the forest, and all other locations in the play. CERRIDWEN enters. She sits and eats greedily and noisily at something she is carrying in her hands. GWYDION enters and speaks to her.*

GWYDION	What are you doing?	1
CERRIDWEN	Eating.	
GWYDION	What?	
CERRIDWEN	A rabbit.	
GWYDION	Is it fresh?	
CERRIDWEN	Almost. The maggots are. Want some?	
GWYDION	No, I don't think so.	
CERRIDWEN	You look like a skeleton. Rags and bones. You ought to eat something.	
GWYDION	Something, yes, but not anything. I'm not a pig.	10
CERRIDWEN	But I am, and I do. *(She takes a bite.)* And it's good. *(She continues to eat greedily.)*	
	(GWYDION shivers and pulls his clothes tighter about him.)	
GWYDION	It's cold. That wind's sharp. Like a knife. Cuts right through to bone. There's nothing to stop it. Flesh too weak, blood too thin. I must be getting old.	
CERRIDWEN	You are old.	

GWYDION	I know. Too old.
CERRIDWEN	Look at you. Gwydion the Wizard. Gwydion the Poet. The Weaver of Webs, Teller of Tales.
GWYDION	Yes. I was once all of those things. There was no miracle I couldn't perform, no wonder I couldn't work. When I spoke my words took wing. I could read the pattern of the stars and the flight of birds. I mapped out the future in men's palms.
CERRIDWEN	Now what are you? A scarecrow. Rags and sticks and bones. No good for anything anymore.
GWYDION	What about you? You're not exactly young yourself.
CERRIDWEN	I'm just in my prime. We pigs wear our years well. And do you know why?
GWYDION	Tell me.
CERRIDWEN	We don't worry. We don't go sweating in the night, fretting about this and that. We don't twist our guts into knots with problems that can't be solved. We don't sing songs and we don't tell tales. We just sleep and eat and –
GWYDION	Yes, all right.
CERRIDWEN	So there you are. That's why I'll live longer than you. *(She eats the last of the rabbit.)* Finished. Delicious. You should have had some.
GWYDION	Listen.
CERRIDWEN	What?
GWYDION	Did you hear that?

20

30

40

When I spoke my words took wing *As a poet, his words were powerful, they rose, as a flock of birds, lifting his hearers with them.*

in my prime *To be in your prime is to be at that age when all your faculties, mental and physical, are at full strength.*

CERRIDWEN	Hear what?
GWYDION	That sound.
CERRIDWEN	No.
GWYDION	A cry. An owl.
CERRIDWEN	Are you scared? Don't be. I'm here to protect you.
GWYDION	She's hunting.
CERRIDWEN	Claws in the skull. Food in the belly. That's the way it goes. *(She starts searching around.)* I wish I could find another rabbit. I'm still hungry. A hedgehog would do. Or a rat . . .
GWYDION	Cerridwen . . .
CERRIDWEN	What? Have you found something to eat?
GWYDION	No.
CERRIDWEN	Oh.
GWYDION	I am still good for something. There is one thing I can do.
CERRIDWEN	Is there?
GWYDION	Telling stories. I can still tell a story.
CERRIDWEN	That won't fill your belly. Or mine.
GWYDION	Let me tell you a story.
	(She stops searching and looks at him.)
CERRIDWEN	Did I hear you right? You want to tell me a story?
GWYDION	Yes.
CERRIDWEN	Why?
GWYDION	Because . . . I want to. And because I can.
CERRIDWEN	What kind of story?
GWYDION	A story of betrayal, treachery and murder. Of dark deeds and magical transformation. Of wonder and enchantment,

50

60

| | love and loss. The story of a woman made from flowers who became an owl . . . | 70 |

CERRIDWEN	The story of a wizard and a pig.
GWYDION	Yes.
CERRIDWEN	That's our story.
GWYDION	Yes.
CERRIDWEN	I already know it. Tell another.
GWYDION	I can't. It's the only story I know. Perhaps it's the only story there is.
CERRIDWEN	What's the point in telling it to me?
GWYDION	There isn't anyone else. Pretend you don't know it.
CERRIDWEN	How can I pretend I don't know it when I'm in it?	80
GWYDION	Use your imagination.
CERRIDWEN	Pigs don't have imaginations.
GWYDION	Please.

(CERRIDWEN considers.)

| **CERRIDWEN** | It won't do any harm, I suppose. And it might take my mind off being hungry. Let me just make myself comfortable. *(She sits.)* That's it. Go on, then. Tell it. |
| **GWYDION** | Very well. |

(He prepares to tell the story. Thinks, considers, begins to grow agitated, says nothing.) 90

CERRIDWEN	Well? I'm waiting.
GWYDION	Yes . . .
CERRIDWEN	Go on.
GWYDION	I . . . don't know where to begin . . .

CERRIDWEN	Try the beginning.
GWYDION	But what is the beginning . . . where did it all start . . . and when . . .?
CERRIDWEN	If you don't know, I'm sure I don't.
GWYDION	It's so difficult . . . trying to find the actual moment when things began . . . the one event that set all the others in motion . . . the spark that started the chain reaction . . .
CERRIDWEN	Start with him. Math. The time he came here. The first time.
GWYDION	Math, King of Gwynedd. Yes.
CERRIDWEN	It was the middle of winter. Colder than it is now.
GWYDION	I remember. The trees stark and bare. Frost on the branches. The earth like iron. A bitter winter.
CERRIDWEN	There was a small fire. You were sitting in front of it, trying to keep warm.
GWYDION	And not doing very well.
	(During the following, MATH enters with LLEW.)
CERRIDWEN	You didn't see him at first. I did. He came through those trees there. The boy was behind him. I grunted. He looked at me. Then he spoke your name.
MATH	Gwydion.
	(GWYDION turns to MATH, narrating.)

100

110

the spark that started the chain reaction *In physics, a chain reaction is a series of events that begin with the splitting of a single atom, and end with a nuclear explosion. It's a series of events, in other words, that once begun cannot be stopped, and lead to some disastrous conclusion. The 'spark' that Gwydion is seeking is the single event that sets all the others happening.*

GWYDION	Math, King of Gwynedd, come to the forest, to see Gwydion the Wizard.	
	(MATH speaks to GWYDION.)	
MATH	You are Gwydion?	120
	(GWYDION speaks to MATH.)	
GWYDION	I am.	
MATH	I've heard much about you. Many marvellous tales.	
CERRIDWEN	And some of them are even true.	
MATH	I hadn't expected . . . this . . . to find you living in such a place . . . in such . . . conditions . . .	
GWYDION	It's how I choose to live. I do not keep the company of men.	
MATH	Rather the company of pigs.	
GWYDION	Cerridwen is a fine companion. We have little to do with the world. Unless the world comes calling on us.	130
CERRIDWEN	*(Narrating.)* As it did then. But what did it want with us? What was it brought the great Lord here?	
	(MATH speaks to GWYDION.)	
MATH	This boy, my son. I've brought him to you. *(MATH speaks to LLEW.)* Go forward, boy. Let him see you.	
	(LLEW steps forward a little.)	
GWYDION	Your son? He's a fine-looking boy.	
MATH	Yes, but he's wild, untrained. He needs educating. I . . . have no skill in such things . . . nor the time. But you perhaps can teach him what he needs to know.	140
GWYDION	And what does he need to know?	
MATH	How to be a king! How to rule the kingdom after I'm gone. You can do this?	

10

GWYDION	I can train him in the skills of war and kingship. I can teach him to ride and hunt and fight. Also I can instruct him in the arts of poetry and music, how to speak gently, and to act with courtesy. I, Gwydion, can do all this. Is it what you want?
MATH	Yes. And one more thing.
GWYDION	What's that?
MATH	Give him a name.
GWYDION	A name? He has no name?
MATH	No. And you shall give him one.
GWYDION	His mother –
MATH	*(Sharply.)* What of her?
GWYDION	It is the mother's right to name her child.
MATH	This mother has forfeited that right! He is my son, alone. He has no mother.
CERRIDWEN	*(Narrating.)* Then we knew there was more to this. Something deeper, something darker. A boy without a mother, a boy without a name. Deep and dark indeed. And he shed no light in that hole.
	(MATH speaks to GWYDION.)
MATH	Will you take him from me? Will you make him a king? Will you give him a name?
GWYDION	I'll take the boy. I'll train him well. As for his name . . .
MATH	The rest is useless without that. A man's nothing without a name.
GWYDION	As for his name – if it exists in the world, I'll find it.
MATH	See that you do. I'll reward you well.
GWYDION	What could you give me that I would desire?

150

160

170

(MATH looks hard at GWYDION for a moment, perplexed.)

MATH See to it.

(He turns to go.)

GWYDION Math.

(MATH stops and turns.) Won't you say goodbye to your son?

MATH He'll be my son when he has a name.

(MATH goes.)

CERRIDWEN And he was gone. As arrogant as he came. Couldn't wait to   180
get back and wash the stench out of his nostrils and the
pig-muck off his boots.

(GWYDION turns to CERRIDWEN.)

GWYDION Was that how it began?

CERRIDWEN For us, yes.

GWYDION It needn't have been. I could have refused. Would things
have turned out differently if I had?

CERRIDWEN Who knows? Does it matter now? Things happen as they
must.

GWYDION Fate, was it, then? Destiny? I could have changed his   190
destiny . . .

CERRIDWEN What's the point in worrying about it? All you get is
indigestion.

GWYDION Poor boy. If he had known then what awaited him. If I had
known. Such harm and pain and hurt. And when he looked
at me, his eyes so full of trust . . .

 *perplexed* Puzzled.

(LLEW turns to GWYDION.)

LLEW	Are you my father, now?

(GWYDION speaks to LLEW.)

GWYDION   For a time, yes, I will be . . . as a father.   200

CERRIDWEN   And I'll be your mother.

LLEW   *(To CERRIDWEN.)* A pig?

CERRIDWEN   Why not? Pigs make good mothers.

GWYDION   *(To LLEW.)* You understand what she says?

LLEW   Yes.

GWYDION   Not everyone can. That's good. Very good. A hopeful start.

LLEW   I don't have a mother. She's dead.

GWYDION   How do you know?

LLEW   I was told. Can I sit by the fire?

GWYDION   Of course.   210

(LLEW sits. During the following, he takes up a stick, and draws with it in the earth. CERRIDWEN speaks to GWYDION.)

CERRIDWEN   But you knew she wasn't dead.

GWYDION   Yes. I knew.

CERRIDWEN   And how did you know?

GWYDION   I'm a wizard. I know everything. Nearly everything. And I knew from the way Math spoke the boy's mother still lived. I knew there was some reason for her not naming him. So, as he sat by the fire, and as the light failed and the darkness crept in, I gazed into the flames, and conjured her, and she   220 stepped from the flames and I learned who she was.

(ARIANHROD enters.)

ARIANHROD   Arianhrod, daughter of Rhiannon, Pryderi's sister. I am this boy's mother.

GWYDION	And this phantom I had conjured, I questioned it, and learned what needed to be known.
ARIANHROD	With my brother, Pryderi, I ruled the kingdom of the West, in our castle overlooking the wide sea. Math saw me and desired me. He asked for my hand but I refused, having no wish to be any man's chattel. Then Math caused a war in which my brother was slain, and me he took by force, to get with his child.
CERRIDWEN	I heard rumours of a war. When I reached the place of battle it was already over. Smoke and blood. The crows and the foxes and the wolves were feasting. I fed well too.
ARIANHROD	Then after he had taken me, and after I had sweated out his child, what once he had desired he loathed. Corrupted, I was cast out. Cast out, I cursed him and his child. 'From me and from no other shall he have his name. And from me his name he shall never have.' So I spoke. And so my words strike true, like blade to throat.

230

240

(ARIANHROD turns away but does not leave the stage.)

CERRIDWEN	A mother's curse. That won't be easy to overcome.
GWYDION	There'll be a way. There's always a way.
CERRIDWEN	Not always. Only his mother can name him, and she won't.
GWYDION	I think she will.
CERRIDWEN	How come?
GWYDION	I'll trick her.

(LLEW looks up at GWYDION.)

this phantom I had conjured *As a wizard, Gwydion has caused Arianhrod's spirit to leave her body, and appear to him.*

any man's chattel *Any man's possession.*

cast out *She was cast out of Math's home.*

| LLEW | Look. I've drawn something. | 250 |

| GWYDION | What is it? |

| LLEW | I don't know. |

| GWYDION | Let me see. |

(GWYDION looks at what LLEW has drawn while CERRIDWEN narrates.)

| CERRIDWEN | You sat there together looking at the pattern he'd scratched in the earth. Your two heads close together, the firelight on your faces. Almost like father and son. |

| GWYDION | It could be a bird . . . |

| LLEW | Or flowers . . . | 260 |

| GWYDION | Yes. It could be . . . |

| CERRIDWEN | And I thought to myself then, this is the last time either of those two is ever going to be really happy. |

(GWYDION stands, and raises LLEW to his feet.)

| GWYDION | But there isn't time for this now. We have more important things to do. We have to make you a king and get you a name. |

| CERRIDWEN | So you trained him and taught him. |

| GWYDION | And taught him well, if I say so myself. |

(During the following, LLEW takes up the stick he was drawing 270 with, and uses it as a spear. He practises with it, then, slowly, takes aim at something, and draws it back over his shoulder.)

| CERRIDWEN | And by the time you'd finished he could fight . . . |

| GWYDION | Wrestle . . . |

| CERRIDWEN | Run . . . |

| GWYDION | Swim . . . |

| CERRIDWEN | Speak poetry . . . |

GWYDION	And write it . . .
CERRIDWEN	Play music . . .
GWYDION	And compose it . . .
CERRIDWEN	He could ride a horse . . .
GWYDION	Wield a sword . . .
CERRIDWEN	Shoot an arrow . . .
GWYDION	Throw a spear.
CERRIDWEN	The only thing he lacked was a name.
GWYDION	And that he would soon have.

280

(ARIANHROD turns and watches LLEW.)

GWYDION For on the beach where we practised, we were not unobserved. From her castle on the clifftop above, Arianhrod watched the boy who was her son . . .

290

CERRIDWEN The boy she didn't know was her son . . .

GWYDION And admired what she saw. Could not resist. Was drawn. As I'd planned.

CERRIDWEN As you'd hoped.

GWYDION As I'd planned.

LLEW Gwydion. Look.

(GWYDION turns to LLEW.)

GWYDION What is it?

LLEW There. Out to sea. A gull riding the waves. You see it?

(GWYDION peers outward.)

300

GWYDION Yes.

LLEW Do you see its head?

GWYDION Yes.

LLEW	Do you see the eye in its head?
GWYDION	Yes . . .
LLEW	With my spear I can pierce that eye.
GWYDION	Can you, now?
LLEW	I can.
ARIANHROD	That's a fine boast, but can you make it good?
	(LLEW turns to ARIANHROD.) **310**
LLEW	I can, lady.
ARIANHROD	Let me see you, then.
LLEW	Very well.

(LLEW takes careful aim again, then mimes throwing the spear.)

There! As I said I would do, I did.

ARIANHROD	I never doubted you. But now your spear's lost.
LLEW	It was worth it to please you, lady. And I can make another.

(ARIANHROD turns to GWYDION. During the following, LLEW returns to CERRIDWEN, sits by her, and draws with the stick in the earth once more.) 320

ARIANHROD	Are you this boy's father?
GWYDION	I'm the only one he calls by that name.
ARIANHROD	He's a boy to be proud of.
GWYDION	I know it, lady.
ARIANHROD	Fair-looking. Very fair. And strong. He has a strong hand.
GWYDION	He does, lady. A very strong hand.
ARIANHROD	And by his look, he's fearless too.
GWYDION	Oh, yes, he's fearless. Like a polecat, aren't you, boy?
ARIANHROD	A polecat? You insult your son giving him such a name.
GWYDION	What name would you give him, then, lady? 330

Like a polecat, aren't you? *A polecat is a large, carnivorous mammal, related to the weasel, stoat and the otter. It is known for its fearlessness. Polecats have become rare in England and, for a time, it was believed they'd disappeared for good, living only in the remoter parts of Wales. But recent research shows that their numbers are rising, and they're returning. One has recently been sighted near Stratford-Upon-Avon in Warwickshire, and I saw one myself while out walking in Shropshire around the time I was writing this play. It seemed to me that, in seeing that creature, I was seeing a part of the ancient past returning, the ancient past I was actually writing about at that time. So I decided to mark the occasion by making this reference to it in the play.*

ARIANHROD	One much more noble than 'polecat'. Lion, I would say.
GWYDION	Do you say so, lady?
ARIANHROD	Yes, I do.
GWYDION	Then a lion he is.
ARIANHROD	Tell me, what's his name?
GWYDION	The name you've given him yourself, lady. Llew Llaw Gyffes. The Lion with the Strong Hand.
ARIANHROD	What was his birth-name?
GWYDION	He didn't have one, lady. His mother refused to give him one. But now she has.

(ARIANHROD starts.)

ARIANHROD	What? What are you saying?
GWYDION	It's cruel of a mother not to name her own child.
ARIANHROD	His mother? This is my son . . . ?
GWYDION	A boy to be proud of.
ARIANHROD	You said you were his father . . .
GWYDION	I said he calls me by that name, which he does. But his true father you know.
ARIANHROD	Yes. I know him. You I do not.
GWYDION	I'm Gwydion, the wizard. The boy's teacher.
ARIANHROD	I pity him, having so deceitful a teacher.
GWYDION	I pity him, having so heartless a mother.
ARIANHROD	You think me heartless? You know what was done to me?
GWYDION	I know.
ARIANHROD	A man such as Math is not fit to be king. Nor any of his blood. He and his kind, they are without honour or respect or shame. They live only to feed their appetites and desires.

340

350

	They will do to the land what was done to me, ravish and defile it, leave it wounded, bleeding. And these are the ones you serve.	360
GWYDION	I serve the boy. I am his teacher. I can do some good . . .	
ARIANHROD	If you believe that you deceive yourself. When I held my brother dying in my arms, I swore this vow: 'Math shall pay. He shall pay the price in full.' So I cursed his son, the son he pushed into me. And now I curse him again. Listen to my words. Tell them to Math. Though this boy that was nameless is now named, he shall never be a true man, never get sons himself. For among those that live now on this earth, he shall never have a lover or wife. So Math's blood shall be barren, and his line die with him.	370
	(ARIANHROD turns and goes.)	
CERRIDWEN	Poor boy. Cursed twice by his mother. I don't see how you're going to get round that one.	
	(GWYDION turns to CERRIDWEN.)	
GWYDION	Neither do I.	
CERRIDWEN	He seems happy enough as he is.	
GWYDION	Perhaps I can't. Perhaps there isn't a way.	
	(MATH enters, angry, determined.)	
MATH	There is! There must be.	
	(GWYDION turns to MATH.)	380
	You have to find a way. For his sake.	
GWYDION	His sake, or yours?	

 **ravish and defile it, leave it wounded, bleeding** *As Arianhrod was raped and corrupted by Math, so, she believes, the earth will also be corrupted by men, if they are allowed complete control of it. In the play, nature, or the earth, is closely linked with the female spirit.*

MATH	It's the same thing. *(He approaches LLEW.)* Look at him, sitting there, scratching in the earth with a stick. Is that what you've been teaching him these past seven years?
GWYDION	I've taught him many things. He has all the skills needed to become a king . . .
MATH	And what use are they if he can't get a wife, if he fathers no sons? What kind of man or king can he be?

(LLEW looks up at MATH.)   390

LLEW	See what I've drawn.
MATH	What?

LLEW	It's a bird, but its feathers are flowers. It comes to me in a dream . . .
MATH	Dreams and drawings! They're nothing! Dirt! Just dirt!

(He stamps out the drawing with his foot, takes hold of LLEW.)

Look at me, boy! Do you know who I am? Have you forgotten me? I'm your father! The king! And when I'm dead you'll be king! The land will be yours! But who'll rule it after you? The land will die! A barren king makes the land **400** barren!

(With a cry, LLEW pulls away from MATH and runs to CERRIDWEN.)

What kind of son have I got? He runs for comfort to a pig!

(He turns to GWYDION.)

Make him a man. Get him a wife.

GWYDION	I can't. His mother's cursed him, laid a destiny on him –
MATH	Are we to be ruled by women? Are we to cower beneath their threats and curses? No! We'll rule this world, we'll take it and shape it to our liking. From now on, we'll make our **410** own destinies. You have power. Use it. Get my son a wife!

(MATH turns and goes. GWYDION stands deep in thought. CERRIDWEN speaks to GWYDION. LLEW draws in the earth again.)

A barren king makes the land barren *A common belief in the ancient world was that the life of the earth was closely linked to the life of the king who ruled it. If the king was barren – if he had no children – the land would be barren too – it would not bring forth crops or fruit, vital to the life of the people.*

His mother's cursed him, laid a destiny on him *Arianhrod's curse has sealed her son's fate. The play is very much concerned with the attempt to break free from destiny, or fate.*

cower beneath *Are we to shrink back in fear from the power of women?*

CERRIDWEN	Gwydion? Let me ask you something.
GWYDION	Mm?
CERRIDWEN	I've often wondered. Why did you help him?
GWYDION	Why?
CERRIDWEN	Yes. You knew no good would come of it.
GWYDION	Did I?

420

CERRIDWEN	You can see into the future. At least, you always claimed you could.
GWYDION	Perhaps my sight wasn't as clear as it used to be. Perhaps I thought, if I found him a wife . . . he'd be . . . happy.
CERRIDWEN	He was already happy.
GWYDION	And there was something in what Math said . . .
CERRIDWEN	You think so?
GWYDION	He was the future . . .
CERRIDWEN	A bleak future. Now tell me the truth.
GWYDION	All right. I wanted to see if I could. I wanted to see if my power was greater than his mother's. To prove myself greater.

430

CERRIDWEN	Pride.
GWYDION	Yes, if you like. Pride.
CERRIDWEN	And you did it.
GWYDION	I did.
CERRIDWEN	You found him a wife.
GWYDION	I made him a wife.
CERRIDWEN	With magic.
GWYDION	With magic.

440

CERRIDWEN	From flowers.

(GWYDION approaches LLEW who is still drawing.)

GWYDION	I had the idea from him. His drawing. Flowers scratched in the dirt. There's the answer, I said. All life is of one essence, springs from the same source. All outward forms illusion only, temporary, provisional. And therefore interchangeable. Capable of . . . change. If one knows the words.
CERRIDWEN	You knew the words.
GWYDION	I gathered them, flowers of oak, broom and meadowsweet, held them in my arms, smelled their fragrance. And from them I called forth a maiden, the fairest maiden that was ever seen or ever walked upon this earth.

450

(BLODEUWEDD has entered. She speaks.)

BLODEUWEDD	Blodeuwedd.

(At her voice, LLEW looks up.)

GWYDION	Woman of flowers.
BLODEUWEDD	Your bride, your wife.

(She holds out her hand to LLEW. LLEW stands and faces her, uncertainly.)

460

GWYDION	Go to her.

All life is of one essence . . . All outward forms illusion only *All that lives is made of the same basic material, has the same force flowing through it. And it is this basic life-force that is important, not its 'outward forms', which are inter-changeable. Knowing this secret, Gwydion is able to cause one 'outward' form of life – flowers – to be changed into another – a woman. This is one of the basic principles behind magic.*

I called forth a maiden *As the basic essence of life contains all forms, Gwydion is able to command one of its forms – that of a maiden – to appear.*

BLODEUWEDD	Come to me.
GWYDION	She's yours.
BLODEUWEDD	I'm yours.

(LLEW goes to BLODEUWEDD, takes her hand.)

LLEW	Mine.

(LLEW and BLODEUWEDD remain still.)

GWYDION	And on the night of their wedding, Math died.
CERRIDWEN	A horrible death, screaming, raving in agony, as if being eaten up from the inside. When they found him he was already rotten. His whole body was alive with worms.

470

GWYDION	So Llew became king, and Blodeuwedd was his queen. And they lived happily –
CERRIDWEN	But not ever after.
GWYDION	No. Not ever after. Though I think for a time –
CERRIDWEN	Not ever.
GWYDION	What?

(During the following BLODEUWEDD looses LLEW's hand and turns from him, facing away, looking out.)

CERRIDWEN	She was never happy. How could she be? She was born to be flowers on the hillside, to grow in the earth, drink the sun and the rain. But you made her flesh, trapped her in a cage of bone and blood. And he held her there, captive. So she hated him for it. And he never knew, poor man. Because he was just that. A man.

480

(BLODEUWEDD sings.)

BLODEUWEDD	My love is dead My love is cold He lies in the ground As the year grows old.

490

LLEW	What's that song?
BLODEUWEDD	An old song.
LLEW	Where did you hear it?
BLODEUWEDD	I don't know. I can't remember. I think I've always known it.
	(Sings.)
	My love is gone My love is lost His kiss is cold As the winter's frost.
LLEW	It's a sad song.
BLODEUWEDD	Is it?
LLEW	Yes. I think so . . .
	(She starts to sing.)
BLODEUWEDD	My love lies deep . . .
LLEW	Blodeuwedd.
	(She stops.)
	Are you happy?
BLODEUWEDD	Happy?
LLEW	Yes. I want you to be happy.
BLODEUWEDD	*(Flat, without expression.)* I am. I am happy.
	(She turns from him and sings.)
	My love lies deep Beneath the earth I wait for the spring To bring his birth.
GWYDION	Then he went away.
CERRIDWEN	His mother sent him a message.

500

510

(LLEW speaks to BLODEUWEDD.)

LLEW   She wants to make peace between us.

BLODEUWEDD   You must go, then.   520

LLEW   I'll return soon.

BLODEUWEDD   It doesn't matter. I'll be waiting for you.

(LLEW goes during the following.)

GWYDION   So he saddled his horse and rode away and came at last to his mother's castle, on the clifftop above the sea. And there he found her waiting for him.

(ARIANHROD enters.)

ARIANHROD   I greeted him, welcomed my son and took him inside. I showed him to a room. In the room was a golden bowl, suspended by silver chains fastened to the air. My son   530 looked into the bowl and there, reflected in the water, he saw the full moon shining. Overcome by thirst he dipped his hand into the water, held it in his cupped palm, lifted it to his lips. And from the moment he drank his body froze, he heard nothing and saw nothing, and stood as if stone, and the enchantment held him fast.

(ARIANHROD remains onstage.)

CERRIDWEN   And on the night of his leaving, Blodeuwedd had a dream.

BLODEUWEDD   A dream of another time, a time before this. I'm on a hilltop, beneath an open sky. I feel the wind in my hair, the dew on   540 my skin, I feel the earth warm and rich beneath me. All about me the world is green and deep, and all is as it was always meant to be. Suddenly it grows dark, a shadow falls, the earth tightens about me, squeezing, crushing. I can't breathe. I think I'm going to die. The wind is a blade of ice at my throat. Then the sun breaks through the darkness, blinding me for a moment. And out of the glare of the sun comes a bird, a hawk, feathers shining. It hangs there a moment above me, then falls, drops, wings folded, comes rushing closer, and the air screams, and it strikes, and I wake – 550

(BLODEUWEDD looks round suddenly, as if waking from her dream.)

GWYDION　　To the sound of a hunting horn.

CERRIDWEN　　The sound of hounds baying down by the river.

GWYDION　　And it was there that she found him, there that she saw him for the first time – Gronw Pebyr, Lord of Penllyn.

(GRONW PEBYR enters. He speaks to BLODEUWEDD.)

GRONW　　I come from the east. There I was hunting with my hounds, and I raised a stag. I gave chase and the beast led me far 560 from my home, over the mountains, through valleys and forests. Here at last, on this hillside, I ran it to ground. Here, by the river, they pulled it down. A magnificent creature. I cut its throat with my knife.

(BLODEUWEDD speaks to GRONW.)

BLODEUWEDD　　There's blood on your hands.

GRONW　　The stag's blood. It will soon wash off in the river . . .

BLODEUWEDD　　No. Not in the river. You must come to my home and wash them there.

GRONW　　I've no wish to trouble you . . . 570

BLODEUWEDD　　It will be no trouble. You've ridden long and far. I'll give you food and fresh clothing. My servants will see to your hounds and your horse. Come.

　**I raised a stag** *He flushed a stag out of hiding.*

GRONW	Who are you, lady?
BLODEUWEDD	My name is Blodeuwedd. I am mistress of this land. And you are my guest.
	(GRONW takes a step towards BLODEUWEDD, then they are both still, facing each other.)
CERRIDWEN	And a bit more than that, after a while.
GWYDION	Yes. It didn't take her long.
CERRIDWEN	It didn't take much to persuade him, either.
GWYDION	He couldn't help himself. Her power was strong.
CERRIDWEN	Fell for her, he did, and didn't think twice.
GWYDION	He was the one she'd been waiting for. The one who'd set her free.

580

CERRIDWEN	Head over heels. Snared and trapped. True love.
GWYDION	But it wasn't love she wanted him for. It was death.

(BLODEUWEDD and GRONW speak.)

BLODEUWEDD	You'll never leave me, now.	
GRONW	No. Never.	590
BLODEUWEDD	You belong to me. My sovereign, my husband, my king.	
GRONW	You have a husband. The land has a king.	
BLODEUWEDD	You'll wear his ring and his crown.	
GRONW	He won't give them up.	
BLODEUWEDD	No. You'll take them.	
GRONW	By force?	
BLODEUWEDD	By force.	
GRONW	Kill him.	
BLODEUWEDD	Yes. Kill him.	

(ARIANHROD speaks. As she does, BLODEUWEDD picks up the 600 *stick and gives it to GRONW. GRONW steps back.)*

ARIANHROD   And at that moment, in the castle by the sea, the golden bowl cracked and the silver chains snapped, and my son stepped free of his enchantment, and returned to his land to meet his death.

(ARIANHROD goes. LLEW enters. He and BLODEUWEDD narrate, speaking to each other.)

LLEW   I met it by the river, in the shape of my wife.

My sovereign *One who rules; a king.*

BLODEUWEDD	I'd heard news of his return, and gone there to greet him.	
LLEW	I stood on one bank, she on the other.	610
BLODEUWEDD	He came on foot, without horse or weapon.	
LLEW	She called to me. I returned her call.	
BLODEUWEDD	His voice sounded clear, joyful, lifting.	
LLEW	I stepped into the river, cold water splashing.	
BLODEUWEDD	It was early morning, the sun was rising.	
LLEW	Light flashed from the surface, a shimmering glitter.	
BLODEUWEDD	Light flashed from the surface, the glare blinding.	

(GRONW steps forward to LLEW, raising the stick as a spear. LLEW stands still as if blinded, transfixed.)

GRONW	And a shadow falling out of the glare.	620
BLODEUWEDD	Out of the stillness, a wind rushing.	
GRONW	Wings folded, dropping.	
BLODEUWEDD	Claws bared for striking.	

(GRONW thrusts the spear into LLEW.)

GRONW	And he strikes!	
BLODEUWEDD	Strikes!	
GRONW	Through and down!	
BLODEUWEDD	He strikes!	
GRONW	Strikes!	
BLODEUWEDD	Through to the bone!	630

(GRONW pushes the spear deep into LLEW. LLEW slowly falls to his knees, gripping the spear. GRONW pulls the spear away. LLEW falls forward.)

GRONW	Then, stillness.

BLODEUWEDD	Birdsong, a soft breeze.
GRONW	Sunlight on the river.
BLODEUWEDD	And blood in the water.

(GRONW drops the spear. He and BLODEUWEDD turn and go. GWYDION steps forward.)

GWYDION	Poor boy, to have a wife who hated him. A wife for his killer. A tragic end for him it would have been, if this had been his end. But it wasn't. There was a magic I'd laid on him that he should not be slain by any man's hand. And that magic worked on him, taking from him his human form, and transforming him into an eagle . . .	640
CERRIDWEN	*(Sharply.)* What?	
GWYDION	And for a whole year he lived as an eagle in the forest –	
CERRIDWEN	An eagle?	
GWYDION	And for a whole year I searched for him until I found him, and called him back to his human shape.	650
CERRIDWEN	What are you talking about?	
GWYDION	The time I found him as an eagle and changed him back into a man.	
CERRIDWEN	That didn't happen.	
GWYDION	Yes, it did! He became an eagle and –	
CERRIDWEN	You're making it up. Or imagining it. Or maybe you dreamed it.	
GWYDION	No –	
CERRIDWEN	It didn't happen like that.	
GWYDION	But I remember –	660
CERRIDWEN	The trouble is, you've told so many stories, you can't tell the difference between what's real and what's made up.	

GWYDION	Is there a difference?
CERRIDWEN	I found him, down by the river. Badly wounded, almost dead. But not quite. I dragged him back here where you were weeping and biting your fingers. No good for anything. I nursed him back to health.
GWYDION	Are you sure? Is that what happened?
CERRIDWEN	Yes.
GWYDION	The eagle –
CERRIDWEN	There was no eagle. There was no magic.
GWYDION	Then there should have been.

(LLEW begins to revive.)

| CERRIDWEN | It took a long time. All through the winter. The wound had gone deep. Into his soul. But he was strong, he fought hard, and with the coming of spring he was recovered. And ready. |

(LLEW is revived now. He speaks to CERRIDWEN.)

| LLEW | Ready for what? |
| CERRIDWEN | *(Indicates GWYDION.)* Ask him. He'll tell you. |

(LLEW turns to GWYDION.)

LLEW	Gwydion?
GWYDION	Yes?
LLEW	What must I do now?
GWYDION	You know.
LLEW	Tell me.
GWYDION	Take back your kingdom. Take your revenge. Kill, as you were killed.
LLEW	Is it necessary?
GWYDION	It is.

670

680

33

LLEW	Why?	690
GWYDION	Blood for blood. It's the law.	
LLEW	Whose law?	
GWYDION	The earth's.	
LLEW	It's a terrible thing, to kill.	
GWYDION	Yes.	
LLEW	If I were to leave them, go away . . .	
GWYDION	You can't! You are the king! Destiny chose you. You must fulfil your destiny.	
LLEW	My destiny. It squeezes me, chokes me, crushes me.	
GWYDION	They too are in pain. As long as she lives in human form. As long as he lives with the memory of your death. Their suffering is on you. Free them of it.	700
LLEW	By killing him.	
GWYDION	Yes.	
LLEW	And her?	
GWYDION	No. She can't be killed. Leave her to me. I'll do what I can.	
LLEW	And me? When I've killed him, will I be free?	
GWYDION	Perhaps.	

(GWYDION takes up the spear and offers it to LLEW.)

	Remember the gull riding the waves. Aim straight. Strike true and clear.	710
LLEW	I will.	

(LLEW takes the spear, turns from GWYDION, and stands on one side of the stage. GRONW enters and stands on the other. He speaks to the audience.)

GRONW	We met at the river, the place of death. I knew he would

return and had been waiting for him. I didn't fear him. I greeted him as a friend. He stood on one side, I on the other. It was evening, the sun was setting, the water was red. I heard a skylark calling, high in the sky. Then he threw his spear and it pierced my heart and darkness and silence came. 720

(GRONW and LLEW remain still. GWYDION goes to LLEW, takes the spear from him, returns to the centre, sits, and begins to draw in the earth.)

CERRIDWEN   Gwydion? Gwydion. What are you doing?

GWYDION   Drawing.

CERRIDWEN   What?

GWYDION   A pattern. The pattern that fixes us all, holds us fast.

CERRIDWEN   The story . . . 730

GWYDION   Is it flowers? Or is it feathers?

CERRIDWEN   The end of the story . . .

GWYDION   There is no end.

CERRIDWEN   You haven't finished . . .

GWYDION   You finish it. I'm tired.

CERRIDWEN   You shouldn't have started it, then.

(He carries on drawing. CERRIDWEN turns to LLEW and GRONW.)

One lay dead. One returned to his home to find his love. But she wasn't there. She'd gone. 740

(BLODEUWEDD enters.)

She'd come here. To find you. Her maker.

(BLODEUWEDD speaks to GWYDION.)

BLODEUWEDD   Help me.

(GWYDION speaks without looking up from his drawing.)

GWYDION	I can't.
BLODEUWEDD	Please.
GWYDION	There's little I can do.
BLODEUWEDD	You made me. You brought me to this. Change me back to what I was.

750

GWYDION	None of us can go back to what we were.
BLODEUWEDD	Who'll help me? Who'll take away this pain?
GWYDION	Your pain will be with you always, a flame in your eyes, a hunger in your heart.
BLODEUWEDD	I want the trees . . . the wind . . .
GWYDION	Go to them. Make your home in the leaves, float your body on the wind.
BLODEUWEDD	Make me flowers again . . .
GWYDION	Not flowers. Feathers. I give you wings. Be a bird. Be flower-face. Be owl.

760

(BLODEUWEDD suddenly freezes. She stands central.)

CERRIDWEN	And so she was. And so she is.
GWYDION	I think it's both.
CERRIDWEN	And he calls for his lost love.
GWYDION	The pattern that holds us. Flowers and feathers.
CERRIDWEN	And she comes to him. But she comes with claws.

GWYDION stops drawing and puts down the stick. CERRIDWEN sits next to him. All are still.

DISCUSSION AND WRITING: In this play, each character causes harm, in some way, to another character. But are any characters more to blame than others? Discuss which characters you think are more blameworthy, and which characters you think are more sympathetic than others. Who do you think is the most sympathetic? Who is the least sympathetic? After your discussions, write a short piece about who you think is the most sympathetic character in the play, and why. Then do the same for the character you think is the least sympathetic.

WRITING: Between them, Cerridwen and Gwydion tell the story of the play. But, although they're telling the same story, they see it from different points of view. This arises mainly from their different characters. Write a short piece about these two, describing their characters, the difference between them (and the similarities) and give examples of their different views of the story.

WRITING: Write a monologue for one of the characters in the story, in which that character tells the story – or a part of the story which concerns that character – from his or her point of view. This could be written in prose or poetry.

ACTING: The play calls for some of the characters to narrate parts of the story as well as speak dialogue. In small groups, take a short section where this happens (a page or two will do) and try acting it out. Pay particular attention to how you show the difference between when a character's narrating, and when he or she is speaking dialogue. After you've tried this out a few times, discuss with others how difficult or easy you found it, and how effective you thought it was.

DISCUSSION: Towards the end of the play, Gwydion says he is drawing a 'pattern that fixes us all, holds us fast'. By this he means that the lives of everyone in the play are controlled by destiny, or fate. Find other examples from the play where characters seem to be 'held fast' by destiny, or where they struggle against destiny. Discuss what you think of this view of human life, and whether you agree with it or not.

WRITING: Arianhrod tells us briefly the story of how Math killed her brother, Pryderi, in war, and then abducted her. If the play had been full-length, this whole episode might have formed part of that longer play. Try outlining and then writing part of this episode. Here are some suggestions:

- Math asks Arianhrod to marry him and she refuses. Pryderi may or may not be in this scene.
- Arianhrod and Pryderi speaking on the night before the battle in which Pryderi is killed. One of them has a sense of coming doom.
- After the birth of their child, Math turns Arianhrod out. Arianhrod curses Math.

DISCUSSION: The play is also concerned with betrayal and revenge. Find incidents or episodes in the play in which someone is betrayed, or someone takes revenge. Do you think the betrayal or the revenge were justified? How does one act of revenge or betrayal lead to another? Do you think the cycle of betrayal and revenge which drives the story ends when the play ends?

WRITING: Which do you think are the three most important episodes in the play? Describe briefly what these are, and say why you think they are important.

WRITING A RADIO PLAY: A longer version of this play was written for and broadcast on radio some years ago. It had a different title: *Kingdom of Crows and Carrion.* Take one of the incidents or episodes from the play, and try writing it as if it's for radio. Some points to remember about radio plays are:

- No-one can see anything. Anything visual has to be created through the spoken word.
- Events and incidents can happen as they do in films – scenes can be much shorter, you can switch from one location to another very quickly, characters don't have to enter and exit like they do onstage, and so on. Think of writing for radio as writing a film for the mind.
- Sound effects can play a very important part in the creation of atmosphere, and in helping to tell the story.

READING AND DISCUSSION: This is an extract from *Math, Son of Mathonwy*, part of which story formed the basis for the play. It's near the end of the story, when Llew has returned from the dead to seek his revenge.

'Blodeuwedd heard that they were coming, took her maidens with her and made for the mountain, and over Cynfael River they made for a court that was on the mountain. But through fear they could not proceed save with their faces looking backwards. And then, never a thing knew they before they fell into the lake, and were all drowned save she alone. And then Gwydion overtook her too, and he said to her: "I will not slay thee. I will do to thee that which is worse; that is," said he, "I will let thee go in the form of a bird. And because of the dishonour thou hast done to Lleu Llaw Gyffes thou art never to dare show thy face in the light of day, and that through fear of all birds; and that there be enmity between thee and all birds, and that it be their nature to mob and molest thee wherever they may find thee; and that thou shalt not lose thy name, but that thou be forever called Blodeuwedd."

'Blodeuwedd is "owl" in the language of this present day. And for that reason birds are hostile to the owl. And the owl is still called Blodeuwedd.'

(Translation by Gwyn Jones and Thomas Jones, from the Everyman edition.)

Discuss the difference and similarities between how the episode is treated here, and how it's treated in the play.

Dramascripts

Dead Man

Dramatised by
DAVID CALCUTT

BACKGROUND TO THE PLAY

Admetus was the son of King Pheres of Pherae. When he was a young man he went on two great adventures: he was one of the heroes who hunted and killed the monstrous Calydonian Boar, and he was one of the Argonauts who sailed with Jason to bring back the Golden Fleece from the distant city of Colchis. It was Jason's uncle, King Pelias of Iolcus, who sent Jason on the quest. When Jason returned, he brought with him not only the Fleece, but also Medea, daughter of King Aeetes of Colchis. Medea practised witchcraft, and she convinced Pelias' daughters that, if they killed their father and then placed his body in a cauldron with certain magic herbs, he would be revived as a young man. Medea demonstrated the truth of this with a sheep, which she killed, and which emerged from the cauldron as a lamb. But, when Pelias' daughters had killed their father, Medea gave them the wrong herbs, and he remained dead. So Jason became King of Iolcus.

One of Pelias' daughters was Alcestis, and she married Admetus when he became King of Pherae, after Pheres abdicated in his favour. But the goddess Artemis had a grudge against Alcestis and, on their wedding night, turned her into a nest of snakes. In horror, Admetus called on Apollo for help, and Apollo persuaded Artemis, his sister, to return Alcestis to her human form. As a further favour, he persuaded the Moerae, or Fates, to grant Admetus the opportunity of avoiding death, if he could find someone willing to take his place.

Apollo favoured Admetus for this reason. Apollo had a son, Asclepius, who was greatly skilled in the arts of medicine. Athene had even given him a drop of the Gorgon's blood, which had the power of restoring the dead to life. Zeus, king of the gods, forbade Asclepius from doing this, but Asclepius disobeyed the command, and used the blood to restore several people to life. To prevent him from continuing, Zeus killed Asclepius with a thunderbolt. Apollo was enraged, but could do nothing against Zeus, who was both king and his father. So instead he turned his wrath on the Cyclopes, the one-eyed giants who had made the thunderbolts for Zeus, and destroyed them. As punishment for this act, Zeus condemned Apollo to work as a slave to a mortal man for a year. The man he chose to be Apollo's master was Admetus. And, during that year, Admetus showed Apollo such honour, kindness and respect, that for ever after Apollo favoured him above all men.

When the time came for Admetus to die, he could find no-one willing to give up their life for him. Seeing his despair, Alcestis gave her life. Some say that the hero Heracles, also a friend to Admetus, went to the land of the dead, wrestled with Death, defeated him, and brought Alcestis back. Others say that Persephone, queen of the dead, would not accept Alcestis's offering, and sent her back to her husband. But whatever the reason, Alcestis was returned from death and re-united happily with her husband.

THE CHARACTERS

(in order of appearance)

ADMETUS *King of Pherae.*

HERMES *a god.*

ALCESTIS *Queen of Pherae.*

MOTHER *of Admetus.*

ANTIOPE *Admetus's old nurse.*

PRONOUNCING THE NAMES

ADMETUS *Ad-mee-tus*

ALCESTIS *Al-sess-tiss*

HERMES *Hur-meez*

ANTIOPE *An-tie-op-ee*

PERSEPHONE *Pur-sef-on-ee*

APOLLO *A-poll-ow*

DEAD MAN

A DMETUS *enters. He stands central.*

ADMETUS	What a wonderful morning! Look at that sky! So clear and blue. Look at that sun! Shimmering gold. And the slopes of the hills there, still in shadow. Swifts skimming the treetops, skylarks climbing up from the fields! Goats bleating, dogs barking. A perfect morning. And, last but not least, it's my birthday!

1

(He remains looking out, as HERMES enters, to one side, dressed in rags, as a beggar. He speaks to the audience.)

HERMES	This man's name is Admetus, and he's king of a city called Pherae, in Thessaly. It's not a very big city, and he's not a very important king. He doesn't command great armies or rule vast tracts of land. Just this one, small city. And, if he appears a little smug, if he seems just a little too pleased with himself, well, that's a common human fault, isn't it? And, as things go, I suppose, a fairly minor one. Because, let's get this straight, right from the start. Admetus is not a bad man. Not a bad man at all.

10

(ALCESTIS enters, carrying a wooden box.)

ALCESTIS	Happy birthday, Admetus.
HERMES	This is his wife. Her name's Alcestis.
ADMETUS	Thank you.

20

43

ALCESTIS	You're awake early.
ADMETUS	I know. I had the most wonderful dream last night. I can't remember a thing about it, except that when I woke up I was laughing! Laughing out loud! And I was wide awake. Even though it was still dark I came out here. I stood and watched the sun rise. And it made me laugh again! I felt so . . . so wide awake! As if I was seeing everything for the first time.
ALCESTIS	It is a beautiful day.
ADMETUS	More than that, Alcestis. I think it's the most perfect day since the beginning of creation.
ALCESTIS	Let me try and make it even more perfect, then.
ADMETUS	Is that possible?
ALCESTIS	I hope so. Here. A gift, for your birthday.
ADMETUS	A gift! You shouldn't have – but I'm glad you did. What is it?
ALCESTIS	Open the box and see for yourself
ADMETUS	*(Opening the box.)* I love presents, and I love surprises. I always have, ever since I was a little boy.
ALCESTIS	I think in your heart you still are a little boy. You've never really grown up. That's one of the things I love about you. Perhaps the thing I love most of all.
	(ADMETUS takes a golden wine goblet out of the box.)
ADMETUS	A wine-cup! Solid gold!
ALCESTIS	I had it made especially for you.

30

40

 **since the beginning of creation** *Since the world was made.*

ADMETUS	And silver inside!
ALCESTIS	There's your name, cut into the stem.
ADMETUS	Yes. I can see.
ALCESTIS	And a vine carved all around the rim.
ADMETUS	Wonderful workmanship. I've never seen anything so exquisite.
ALCESTIS	I wanted to give you something special, and I couldn't think what else.
ADMETUS	It's perfect. A perfect gift for a perfect day.
ALCESTIS	You like it? Really?
ADMETUS	Of course I do! I shall never drink my wine out of anything else. Thank you, Alcestis. Thank you very much.
	(ADMETUS's MOTHER enters.)

50

MOTHER	Good morning, my son, and a happy birthday to you.	6(
HERMES	And this is Admetus's mother.	
ADMETUS	Mother. How are you? Where's Father?	
MOTHER	Have you forgotten? He's not well. He wanted to come and see you, but the doctor said he wasn't to leave his bed.	
ADMETUS	Oh, yes, of course. He's not . . . very ill, is he?	
MOTHER	No. Not very ill. Just old. When you're old even a slight chill can knock you off your feet. But your father's a strong man, and I'm sure he'll recover soon.	
ADMETUS	Yes, of course he will.	
MOTHER	He is rather miserable, though. I'm sure he'd appreciate a visit from you . . .	7(
ADMETUS	I'll go and see him in just a few minutes, Mother. But let me show you this first. See what my dear Alcestis has given me for my birthday.	
	(He shows her the cup.)	
MOTHER	It's beautiful.	
ADMETUS	She had it specially made.	
MOTHER	*(To ALCESTIS.)* You're always so very thoughtful, Alcestis. My son's lucky to have you as his wife. I hope he appreciates you.	8(
ALCESTIS	He does. Just as I appreciate him.	
ADMETUS	You see, Mother? We appreciate each other, as a loving husband and wife should. And the times we can show that appreciation most are special occasions – like birthdays . . .	
MOTHER	I know what you're hinting at. I have a gift for you as well. In fact, it's from your father. I said he should give it to you himself – when you go to see him. But he insisted I give it to you straight away. Here.	

(She gives him a ring.) 90

ADMETUS A ring . . .

MOTHER Not just any ring. It's your family ring. Your father had it from his father, and he had it from his father, and so on, right back to the beginning of your line. It's hundreds of years old. And priceless, of course. *(She puts the ring on his finger.)* There.

ADMETUS Mother . . . I just . . . I don't know what to say . . .

MOTHER I'm sure you'll think of something. And when you do, you can tell your father.

ADMETUS I will . . .

ALCESTIS Now you can truly say you're King of Pherae, Admetus. And 100 when we have a son, and he's grown, you can pass the ring on to him.

ADMETUS Yes. Yes, I can. This is truly a cause for celebration. And I've had the most marvellous idea. Let's have breakfast outside, in the garden. An early morning picnic, in honour of my birthday, and the giving of this ring.

ALCESTIS It's a good idea, Admetus. It will be lovely to sit and eat on the grass beneath the trees.

ADMETUS You'll join us, Mother?

MOTHER I'd like to. But your father . . . 110

ADMETUS Surely he won't be able to if he's ill.

MOTHER I mean I ought to sit with him. I don't like to leave him alone for long . . .

ADMETUS Ask one of the servants to sit with him, then. It won't be for long. Please, Mother. This is a special occasion, and I am your only son . . .

MOTHER Very well. But only for a little while. And because you are my only son.

(She moves away.)

You will go and see him, won't you, Admetus?   **120**

ADMETUS   I'll go straightaway, before we eat. I want to thank him myself for this ring.

(MOTHER goes.)

ALCESTIS   I must go too.

ADMETUS   Why? Where?

ALCESTIS   If we're to eat outside, arrangements must be made. Give me the wine-cup. I'll have it filled for you with our very best wine.

ADMETUS   Thank you. I'll see you soon, then. When everything's been made ready.   **130**

ALCESTIS   Yes. When everything's been made ready.

(She moves off.)

ADMETUS   Alcestis. I'm very happy, you know.

ALCESTIS   Yes, Admetus. I know. And so am I.

(She goes.)

ADMETUS   Such a fine, clear morning. I think I must be the happiest man in the world.

(He remains still as HERMES speaks.)

HERMES   The happiest man in the world. Yes. At this moment he is. Let him savour it. He may never taste such happiness again.   **140**

(ANTIOPE enters.)

ANTIOPE   Admetus – Master . . .

HERMES   Now this is Admetus's old nurse, Antiope.

ADMETUS   Good morning, Antiope. How are you today?

ANTIOPE   Very well, master, considering.

HERMES	She looked after him as a baby, raised him as a child, and she loves him probably even more than his mother.
ADMETUS	Considering what, Antiope?
ANTIOPE	Considering my age, master.
ADMETUS	Your age? You're not old, are you, Antiope?
ANTIOPE	Don't tease me, Admetus. You know I am.
ADMETUS	I don't know anything of the kind. Look at me. Let me see your face. You're not old, Antiope, and you never will be. I think you may well live for ever.
ANTIOPE	Don't say such things, master! Only the gods are immortal. We humans certainly aren't, as my creaking bones testify. Live for ever! God forbid. What a curse that would be.
ADMETUS	A curse? More of a blessing, I'd say. Knowing that every day, for the rest of time, you'd wake to see mornings like this one.
ANTIOPE	You'd tire of them eventually.
ADMETUS	Not me. I'd never tire of life. Although I must say, Antiope, I do feel a little older today.
ANTIOPE	Do you?
ADMETUS	Yes. I'm definitely feeling my age.
ANTIOPE	I must admit, now I look at you, your face does have a few more lines . . .
ADMETUS	What?
ANTIOPE	And those are definitely wrinkles under your eyes . . .

150

160

 **Only the gods are immortal** *Only the gods never die.*

ADMETUS	Wrinkles?	170
ANTIOPE	And there is a touch of grey in your hair . . .	
ADMETUS	My hair! Grey! It can't be! I won't believe it! Fetch me a mirror! Let me see for myself . . .	
ANTIOPE	But that's all probably because it's your birthday.	
ADMETUS	You've been having me on.	
ANTIOPE	That's right. You were always an easy one to tease.	
ADMETUS	You hadn't forgotten my birthday at all . . .	
ANTIOPE	Forget your birthday! Me, who raised you and brought you up! How could you ever think I'd forget your birthday?	
ADMETUS	And have you got me a present?	180
ANTIOPE	Yes. I was going to give it to you later – but, seeing as you're awake so early, you can have it now. I'll just go and fetch it.	
ADMETUS	Thank you . . .	
ANTIOPE	Don't thank me until you see it.	
ADMETUS	I'm sure I will. I'm going to stand here with my eyes closed, just like I used to when I was a boy, and when you come back you can count to three, and then I'll open them – and see my present!	
ANTIOPE	If you wish. But you haven't done that for years . . .	
ADMETUS	I know – but I feel so excited today. I don't know why. Somehow I feel it's particularly special. As if something wonderful is waiting to happen.	190
ANTIOPE	You don't have a temperature, do you? You seem a little too excited – feverish, perhaps . . .	
ADMETUS	I'm perfectly well, Antiope. I've never felt better. Now, stop fussing and go and bring me my present!	
ANTIOPE	Close your eyes, then.	

ADMETUS	Oh, yes. Right.
	(He closes his eyes.)
ANTIOPE	And don't open them till I've come back and counted to three.
ADMETUS	I won't.
	(ANTIOPE goes. ADMETUS stands with his eyes closed. HERMES steps forward.)
HERMES	And now it's time for me to make my entrance. And who am I? A common beggar? No beggar, I assure you, and in no way common. My name you'll find out in a moment. As he will. And the reason for my coming here to visit him. Which is not to wish him a happy birthday.
	(HERMES walks towards ADMETUS. He stands in front of him and counts.)
	One. Two. Three. Open your eyes for a big surprise.
	(ADMETUS opens his eyes. He stares at HERMES in shock.)
ADMETUS	Who are you? How did you get in here? You look like a beggar. What's a beggar doing in my palace? Or are you a thief? Come to rob me, have you? We'll soon see about that! Get out of here, you rogue, or it'll be the worse for you!
HERMES	You threaten me, do you?
ADMETUS	Yes, I do!
HERMES	You'll do me harm?
ADMETUS	I will.
HERMES	With what?
ADMETUS	With this.
	(He draws a knife from his belt.)
HERMES	A knife. Very brave. Go, then. Do your worst.

200

210

220

ADMETUS	You've asked for this – ah – !
	(He cries out in pain and drops the knife.)
	My knife – it burned my hand –
HERMES	I know.
ADMETUS	You did that?
HERMES	Just a little party trick – to let you know I am no thief or beggar. Pick up your knife. Put it back in your belt. Don't worry. It won't burn you now.
	(ADMETUS picks up the knife.)
ADMETUS	Who are you?

230

 **Just a little party trick** *To Hermes, the miraculous power he has just displayed is nothing more than a trick he might play at a party. As a god, his true powers are much more powerful than this.*

HERMES	Why don't you try and guess?
ADMETUS	A god?
HERMES	That's right. But which one?
ADMETUS	I don't know – Zeus? The great king? The All-Father?
HERMES	Sorry. No. I'm Hermes.
ADMETUS	The messenger.
HERMES	Among other things.
ADMETUS	You've brought me a message from the gods?
HERMES	One of them has sent you a message, yes.
ADMETUS	It must be something of great importance.
HERMES	It is – for you.
ADMETUS	I knew this day felt special. From the moment I woke I felt it – a tingling in the air, everything sharper, clearer. Now I know why. Some god has chosen this day to favour me. A god from heaven beckons me . . .
HERMES	Not quite from heaven.
ADMETUS	What?
HERMES	My message doesn't come from heaven.
ADMETUS	But you said –
HERMES	A god has called you.
ADMETUS	If not from heaven, where? Beneath the sea! Poseidon –
HERMES	No.
ADMETUS	There's nowhere else.
HERMES	Think again.

240

250

(ADMETUS *thinks. Then he stares in growing fear at* HERMES *as realisation comes to him.*)

260

ADMETUS	No . . . !
HERMES	I think you've got it now.
ADMETUS	Hades . . . ?
HERMES	He's the one.
ADMETUS	God of the Dead!
HERMES	Yes. Your god from now on. That's what I've come to tell you. I should have come straight out with it, I suppose, instead of teasing you. But I just can't help it. It's my nature. Still, here's the message plain and clear. Hades calls you. Today's your death-day. Today's the day when you must die.
ADMETUS	It can't be!
HERMES	I'm afraid it is.
ADMETUS	But why? Why today?
HERMES	Each man and woman born has an allotted time on earth, a certain span of years, no more, no less. Their death-day's fixed by fate from the moment of their birth. And when that last day comes, then I arrive to lead them from this world to the next. Your day is here, and so am I.
ADMETUS	But today, of all days. My birthday!
HERMES	A particularly wicked twist of fate, I must admit. And rare, quite rare. I think you can rest assured, if only for that, people will remember you.
ADMETUS	I don't want to be remembered! I want to live!
HERMES	You've had your life. It's done. And it's been a good life.

270

280

A particularly wicked twist of fate *A twist of fate is when something seems to happen with a purpose, usually something not very pleasant. The fact that Admetus's death-day is to be the same as his birth-day is, according to Hermes, a 'wicked' example of this.*

Parents who've doted on you, a wife who's loved you. No hardship, no great sorrows. If you were to live any longer, who knows what might happen? Who can tell what trials and heartaches might lie ahead? Be happy to quit while the going's good. And on such a fine day too. You couldn't ask for better. 290

ADMETUS When am I – what's the exact hour appointed for my death?

HERMES Now. There's no time like the present.

ADMETUS I won't go with you. I refuse to go.

HERMES I'm afraid you have no choice.

ADMETUS But I do, you see. I do. Your sudden arrival made me forget. Now it's come back to me. The god Apollo has given me a choice.

HERMES Apollo? What dealings have you had with him? 300

ADMETUS Some years ago he came and worked for me.

HERMES Worked for you? A god your servant? What kind of story's this?

ADMETUS A true story. He offended Zeus, and as his punishment, Zeus bound him for a month to work for a mortal. That mortal was me. For that month Apollo looked after my stables.

parents who've doted on you *Parents who've paid you every attention.*

Poseidon . . . Apollo . . . Zeus *The Ancient Greeks believed that creation was ruled by a large family of gods. Here are three of them. Zeus is king of the gods and ruler of heaven and earth. Poseidon is his brother, and rules the sea and the rivers. Apollo is one of Zeus's sons, by the goddess Leto, and is the god, among other things, of prophecy (foretelling the future) and poetry. Hermes is another son of Zeus, but by a different mother, the goddess Maia. As well as being heaven's messenger, he also invented the lyre (a stringed instrument, which he gave to Apollo) and is the god of tricksters and thieves.*

mortals *People who are mortal, who die. Humans.*

HERMES	I seem to remember some such incident . . .
ADMETUS	But here's the important part. Even though he was bound to me, I treated the god well, showed him all proper respect. Because of that, on the day he left, Apollo made a gift to me. 310
HERMES	Go on. What was it.
ADMETUS	He said that when the time came for me to die, if I could find someone to take my place – someone who'd willingly die instead of me – then death would pass me by. I'd keep my life.
HERMES	I know nothing of this! Are you sure it's true?
ADMETUS	Would I be lying?
HERMES	You might – to try and trick me . . .
ADMETUS	If you don't believe me ask the god himself. 320
HERMES	I intend to. One moment while I commune with heaven.
	(He closes his eyes for a few seconds, then opens them again.)
	You're right. You speak the truth. Apollo made that gift to you.
ADMETUS	There! You see?
HERMES	Trust Apollo, to pull a stunt like that. A bright god, shining with poetry and music. But with cruelty as well. Like a cat with a bird is Apollo with mortals. He plays with them, gives them hope of freedom – then snap! He strikes.
ADMETUS	What do you mean? Does he mean to break his word? 330
HERMES	Oh, no. Apollo would never do that. But can't you see the bitterness of his gift? Find someone to take your place, he says, and you won't have to die. But where will you find someone who'll do that? Who'll go willingly to their deaths so that another might live? Not a single human soul. Life's

	too precious to you all. You've proved that yourself. So, he offers you this chance of life, knowing all the time you're bound to lose it. That's real heavenly cruelty. It's divine.
ADMETUS	But if I do find someone –
HERMES	You won't. 340
ADMETUS	You're bound at least to let me try.
HERMES	Why prolong your agony? Why give Apollo the satisfaction of watching you suffer? The way to pay him back is to scorn his gift, fling it aside, walk bravely to your death.
ADMETUS	No. I want my chance. Give me until the sun sets.
	(HERMES pauses for a moment, considering.)
HERMES	Very well. If you insist. You have this day's grace. But when the first shadows of evening fall, I'll be here again. And I shan't be leaving alone.
	(HERMES turns away from ADMETUS and speaks to the 350 *audience.)*
	Hope. That's the food you mortals feed on. All that sustains you, it seems. Hope, you call it. I call it self-deception. Let's wait around and see how this one fares. See just how many refusals it will take to make him finally face the truth. I fear it will be a long and bitter process. And who'll be the first to start it off?
	(ADMETUS's MOTHER enters. ADMETUS turns to her.)
	Ah, yes. His dear old mother. Come to see why he hasn't been to see his father yet. 360
ADMETUS	I'm sorry, Mother – but something's just happened – something important –
MOTHER	More important than your father?
ADMETUS	Yes – I mean –

MOTHER	I wonder sometimes just how much you really care about either of us. It's all take and no give as far as you're concerned. And always has been. I suppose it comes of you being an only child. We've spoiled you . . .
ADMETUS	Mother –
MOTHER	. . . and this is what we get for it. Ingratitude and selfishness. There's your poor father lying ill in bed, and you can't even find a few minutes to go and see him, not even to thank him for giving you his ring . . .
ADMETUS	*(Shouts.)* Will you be quiet!
	(She looks at him, shocked.)
	I'm sorry, but you must listen to me. There's something I have to tell you. And something I have to ask.
	(They freeze.)
HERMES	So he tells her that today he's going to die. And of course she's very upset. And then he tells her about Apollo's gift, and the chance he has of avoiding his death.
ADMETUS	So you see, Mother, if I can find someone to take my place, there'll be no need for me to die.
MOTHER	But where will you find such a person?
ADMETUS	There must be someone – someone who loves me enough to sacrifice themselves for me.
MOTHER	You think so?
ADMETUS	Someone who has lived their life – who's approaching the end of it – has only a short time left – and would happily give up that time . . .
MOTHER	*(Suddenly realising who he means.)* Do you have someone in mind?
ADMETUS	Someone, perhaps someone who isn't in the best of health – whose life is one of suffering.

370

380

390

58

MOTHER	You wicked boy! You mean your father! You want your father to die!
ADMETUS	I don't want him to die – if it could be avoided – but he is ill . . .
MOTHER	Not so ill that he won't recover! Not so ill that he can't enjoy to the full what time he has left!

400

ADMETUS	But what about me? What about the time I have left? I'm a young man. There are years ahead of me! Decades! Are they all to be thrown away, wasted!
MOTHER	If it's the will of the gods!
ADMETUS	One of the gods has given me the chance to have those years back! It's only fair! You and Father have had your lives! Please, Mother. Let me at least ask Father . . .
MOTHER	No, you wretched child! I won't let you go near him!
ADMETUS	If not Father, then you!
MOTHER	Me?

410

ADMETUS	Yes! You always used to say a mother cares more for her children than for herself. Prove it, now. Show how much you love your only son. Give up your life for me!
MOTHER	I'll tell you what I'll do. I'll give you the best funeral money can buy. I'll build a monument on your tomb so that your name won't be forgotten. And every year, on this day, the day of your birth and the day of your death, prayers will be said, and songs sung in your honour. All that I'll do for you, my son. But die for you, I won't.
ADMETUS	Mother . . . !

420

 **the will of the gods** *What the gods have decided will happen.*

MOTHER	Let that be an end to it! There's no more to be said!
	(She turns and goes. ADMETUS stares after her. HERMES speaks to the audience.)
HERMES	What did I say? Am I right so far? Now perhaps the truth begins to reveal its terrible face. If not even his mother will give her life for him, who else will?
	(ANTIOPE enters, carrying a cloak.)
	Perhaps her. His old and faithful nurse. Surely she'll be willing.
ANTIOPE	Admetus.
ADMETUS	What?
ANTIOPE	You've cheated. Opened your eyes and spoiled the surprise. You were always the same. Never mind, here it is, my birthday gift to you. A cloak. Well? Do you like it?
ADMETUS	Yes . . .
ANTIOPE	You don't seem very sure. Is that all you can say? Just 'yes'?
ADMETUS	Antiope . . .
ANTIOPE	I know it isn't much. Nothing gold or silver. I'm too poor to afford anything like that. Just a simple cloak. But I did weave it myself, and you might show a little more appreciation . . .
ADMETUS	I like it very much. Thank you. But, if you would like to give me something really special – something that would mean more to me than anything else – then now you have the chance.
ANTIOPE	Something special? Meaning this cloak isn't?
ADMETUS	Something even more special than this excellent cloak. A rare gift indeed. And one that would make me the happiest man alive.
	(They freeze.)

430

440

450

HERMES	So he tells what this gift is – the gift of his life.
ANTIOPE	Your life? I don't understand. That's a gift you already have.
HERMES	So then he tells her the whole story, explains everything – and what it is he wants her to do.
ANTIOPE	Oh, that's a terrible thing, Admetus. Terrible. I don't know what to say. To think I should have lived to see you born into the world, to have raised you from a child to a grown man – and that I'll live to see you die out of the world as well. Terrible. Awful. It's almost too much for an old woman to bear.

460

ADMETUS	You don't have to bear it, Antiope. You don't have to see me die. That's what I'm trying to tell you. You can leave this world in the happy knowledge that I'm alive and well, and will continue to be so for many years yet.
ANTIOPE	So you say. But I'm not so sure. Remember what I've often said to you? Each man and woman's life is their own – even the life of a slave like me. One life can't be exchanged for another – and neither can a death.
ADMETUS	But in my case it can. I can exchange my death – with someone who's willing.

470

ANTIOPE	Yes, you see. That's the point. Only if someone is willing.
ADMETUS	Meaning you're not.
ANTIOPE	Admetus – my dear Admetus. I'll weep for you . . .
ADMETUS	It's not your tears I want!
ANTIOPE	And always remember you fondly. And this cloak I've woven for you – I'll place it on your body as a shroud.

shroud *A sheet for covering the dead when they're placed in the grave.*

ADMETUS	Antiope, I beg you –
ANTIOPE	Poor boy. You really should have gone with Hermes straight away. I hate to see you suffering like this, prolonging the agony of the inevitable. In fact, I can't bear to stay any longer –

480

ADMETUS	No, please do stay –
ANTIOPE	I'm afraid I'll break down. Let me go. Do me this kindness. Let me go and be alone with my tears.

(ANTIOPE turns to go.)

ADMETUS	Antiope, wait . . .

(She stops, turns back, takes the cloak from ADMETUS, and goes.)

Antiope!

HERMES	He calls but she's gone. She doesn't come back. He's alone. As each man is when it's time to face his death.

490

(ADMETUS speaks out.)

ADMETUS	No! I will not face it! I've been given this chance! It can't be for nothing. There must be someone, someone here in the palace or the city, who'll willingly exchange their life for mine!

(ADMETUS stands central as HERMES speaks.)

HERMES	And off he goes to try and find this person. From room to room he runs, down every passage and corridor, then outside through the courtyards and gardens, asking everyone he meets . . .

500

(ADMETUS calls out.)

ADMETUS	Will you give your life for mine?
HERMES	But there's no-one . . .
ADMETUS	No-one?

HERMES	No-one. No-one in the whole palace. So he leaves the palace, goes out into the city, runs wildly among the streets of Pherae, asking anyone and everyone . . .
ADMETUS	Who'll give their life?
HERMES	Bakers, butchers, blacksmiths . . .
ADMETUS	Who'll die for me?
HERMES	Weavers, wine-merchants, wheelwrights . . .
ADMETUS	Who loves their king enough to lay down his life? Or her life?
HERMES	Old men and old women, young boys and young girls. Anyone and everyone. But always the answer's the same . . .
ADMETUS	No?
HERMES	No.
ADMETUS	No-one?
HERMES	No-one.
ADMETUS	I can't believe it! It can't be true!
HERMES	But it is true. He has to believe it.
ADMETUS	I won't! I won't believe it! There must be someone some-where! *(He cries out.)* God Apollo! You granted me this gift! I call upon you now! Make good your promise! Mark some other for death! Let one be found who'll willingly die for me!
HERMES	And there's thunder in the sky. A deep booming roll. Flash of white lightning above the mountains. It seems Apollo's answered him. And called to me. A bargain's to be made, a deal delivered. And Admetus, for the time being, is reprieved.

(HERMES goes. ADMETUS speaks to himself.)

ADMETUS	Did Apollo hear me? Will he grant my request? I thought for a moment, when I heard the thunder – the god's voice. But I was wrong. It was just thunder. Or Apollo's laughter.

510

520

530

Hermes spoke the truth. I should have gone with him this morning. It would be all over and done with. Now I have to wait for him to come, when the sun sets. And it's setting now. The land darkening, the western sky turning red. The colour of blood. I've never known the sun sink so fast. The world must be in a hurry to be rid of me. A few last rays, a   540
last glimmer of light – gone. Darkness. And soon he'll be here, to take me to the place where no sun ever shines . . .

(ANTIOPE enters.)

ANTIOPE   Admetus –

(ADMETUS starts, turns and sees her.)

ADMETUS   You! I thought it was – What do you want? Come for a last look at me? Or have you changed your mind?

ANTIOPE   No –

ADMETUS   I didn't think so. Take one last look, then. Here I am. Now you see me, soon you won't.   550

ANTIOPE   Admetus, listen –

ADMETUS   Strange that it should be you who's the last person to see me alive. And fitting too. You raised me, after all.

ANTIOPE   Will you listen to me – ?

ADMETUS   The only one. Everyone else avoids me. My mother, my father, even my wife.

ANTIOPE   Yes, your wife –

ADMETUS   She's the only one I haven't asked. I couldn't have borne to have her refuse me. As it is I'll never know. So at least I'll die with one illusion left . . .   560

ANTIOPE   It's about her, about Alcestis . . .

ADMETUS   Have you seen her, Antiope? Will you tell her goodbye from me?

ANTIOPE   I think it's already too late for that.

ADMETUS	Too late? What do you mean?
ANTIOPE	I've seen your wife – but I don't think anyone will see her again.
ADMETUS	She's gone away, you mean? Has her grief at my death proved too much for her?
ANTIOPE	She's gone away, yes . . .
ADMETUS	Where? Did she tell you?
ANTIOPE	I know where she's gone. And I know why she's gone. It's not what you think. Listen. I'll tell you. She heard the news of your death, of course. Heard about the gift Apollo had granted you – and how you couldn't find anyone to accept that gift . . .
ADMETUS	I understand now. She's gone away because she thought I might ask her . . .
ANTIOPE	No. It's not that. Not that at all. Listen to me. And don't interrupt.

570

580

(As ANTIOPE tells her story, ALCESTIS enters on another part of the stage, enacting what ANTIOPE describes.)

	All day she shut herself away in her room. Locked the door, wouldn't let anyone in. In grief and mourning, I supposed. As evening approached, I thought I ought to try and see her. To tell you the truth I was worried about her.
ADMETUS	Worried about her, but not about me.
ANTIOPE	I thought nothing could be done for you. Don't interrupt me again. I went to her room, and this time found the door was open. I went in, and saw her standing at the window. She was dressed in her finest clothes – the clothes she wore on your wedding day. And she was singing softly to herself. She turned as I entered – and her face was shining – she looked more beautiful than she's ever looked before – and she was smiling.

590

ADMETUS	Smiling? At my death?
ANTIOPE	No. At her own.
ADMETUS	What? What do you mean? Tell me!
ANTIOPE	I'm trying to. I asked her why she was smiling, why she was singing – why was it she seemed so happy – and she answered me.

(ALCESTIS speaks to ANTIOPE.)

ALCESTIS	Because today I've given my husband the greatest gift. The gift he cherishes most. I've given him his life.

(ANTIOPE speaks to ALCESTIS.)

ANTIOPE	His life – but how, my lady? You know he's going to die today . . .
ALCESTIS	He thinks he is, but he's not. The sun will sink, night will come, and he'll still be living. And when that night has

600

	passed, he'll see the rising of the sun. And he'll see it rise	610
	the next day, too, and the day after, and the day after that.	
	And so on, sunrise after sunrise, for years to come.	

ANTIOPE   It's not possible. Unless – unless he's found someone to take his place . . .

ALCESTIS   He has.

(ANTIOPE turns to ADMETUS.)

ANTIOPE   And by the look on her face – the strange light in her eyes – I knew – I knew what she was going to do – and tried to stop her – implored her not to – to think again . . .

(ALCESTIS speaks to ANTIOPE.) 620

ALCESTIS   It's no good, Antiope. I've decided.

(ANTIOPE turns to ALCESTIS.)

ANTIOPE   No, my lady. I beg you. Don't say the words.

ALCESTIS   They're already spoken in my thoughts. Now I repeat them aloud, for the gods to hear. I shall die in my husband's place. I shall die, so that he may live.

(ANTIOPE turns back to ADMETUS. As she speaks to him, HERMES enters and walks over to ALCESTIS.)

ANTIOPE   And as she spoke, there was a roll of thunder. Lightning flashed. The whole room was filled with light. And another 630 figure stood there. A god, I could tell. He held his hand out to her, and she took it. Then the light grew brighter, so bright I couldn't see. It hurt my eyes. Then the light faded. The room was in shadow. And she was gone.

(HERMES has taken ALCESTIS by the hand and led her offstage.)

ADMETUS   Gone?

ANTIOPE   The room was empty. Your dear wife's body and soul, gone to the dead land.

ADMETUS	Alcestis – she did this for me – the one person I didn't ask.	640

ANTIOPE   Only because you were afraid that she'd say no. You thought she was like all the others.

ADMETUS   I never dreamed – never imagined . . .

ANTIOPE   All my life I've served this family. You I've looked after from the day you were born, like a second mother, and you've been as dear to me as if you were my own child. When you told me you were to die it broke my heart. And when you asked me to take your place, I thought it was the shock that made you say it. Then I heard you'd asked your mother. That brought me up sharp. And later, when I discovered   650
you'd been running round the city like a madman, trying to find anyone who'd take your place, begging on your knees – weeping – suddenly I felt I didn't know you anymore – felt as if I'd never known you. And now this has happened. Your wife, Alcestis – who never did anyone any harm – whose only fault was loving you too much – now she's dead. And I say it's down to you. You killed her, just as if you'd taken a knife and cut her throat. Her death lies on you, Admetus, and as long as you live, I pray you'll suffer and do penance for it. I'd make sure you did if I was here,   660
but I won't be. I can't serve you any longer. I can't stay in this place. Old woman that I am, I have to leave. What I've witnessed today has left a bad taste in my mouth. And I think I must go far from here before I can wash it out.

(ANTIOPE turns and walks away.)

ADMETUS   Antiope!

(She stops for a moment, but does not turn, and goes. ADMETUS calls again.)

Antiope!

*(On another part of the stage, HERMES enters. When he speaks,   670
ADMETUS does not hear him.)*

HERMES	He calls her name, but she doesn't come back. And the one who does arrive, he can't see.

(ADMETUS calls again.)

ADMETUS	Antiope!
HERMES	Because I'm here now, not with a message for him, but a message for you. To set your minds at ease. Alcestis's death will be rejected. Persephone, Queen of the Dead, will not accept her. 'No wife,' she'll say, 'should give up her life for her man. Such sacrifice is not required.' And she'll send Alcestis back. And with tomorrow's sunrise they'll be re-united.

680

(ADMETUS calls.)

ADMETUS	Come back here! Come back!
HERMES	But that's yet to come. For him, it hasn't happened yet. And this is the moment when we'll last see him. This moment of darkness and despair. This moment of truth. This moment that will live in him for ever.

(ADMETUS calls again.)

ADMETUS	Come back to me!

690

HERMES	His voice echoes through the palace. But no-one answers him. No-one comes.
ADMETUS	As if the palace is empty.
HERMES	He goes to the window and looks out. It's night. The city lies in darkness. Not a single light burns. Not a single shadow moves through any street.
ADMETUS	As if the whole city is deserted. As if I'm the only living person here.
HERMES	The only living person in the entire world.
ADMETUS	That can't be. It's ridiculous.

700

69

HERMES	So he listens. And there's no sound. No sound from anywhere. Complete stillness. Utter silence. Not even the beating of his own heart. And a terrible fear begins to creep over him. A cold fear, like ice in his veins, freezing his blood.
ADMETUS	It's impossible.
HERMES	He speaks aloud, and his voice is flat.
ADMETUS	Not me.
HERMES	Flat and thin and dull – and dead.
ADMETUS	No . . .
HERMES	The voice of a dead man.
ADMETUS	No! No! I'm alive. God's gift. Life. Mine. To have. To hold. To grip. For ever.

710

(ADMETUS stands central, his hands gripped into fists.)

HERMES	See him as he is now, in the dark room, in the silent palace, in the empty city. He doesn't speak. He doesn't move. He stares at nothing. See him as he will always be. Ears deaf. Eyes blank. Heart cold. A dead man.

HERMES goes and ADMETUS stands alone. Lights fade on him.

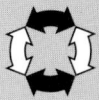 **DISCUSSION AND WRITING:** Why do you think the play is called *Dead Man*? Look at the very end of the play. What has happened to Admetus? Hermes calls him a 'dead man'? But in what way is he dead? Discuss this in small groups, or as a class, then write a short piece about why you think the play has this particular title.

WRITING: If you were going to be in this play, and had the choice, which character would you want to play? Write a short piece saying what it is you find appealing about this character.

WRITING: How would you describe Admetus at the start of the play? What kind of character is he? Does your view of him change as the play continues? And has he changed in any way by the time the play ends? Find incidents in the play that tell us something about Admetus's character, and use these to write a piece about him.

WRITING: Write a monologue for Alcestis in which she says why it was she decided to give up her life for her husband.

WRITING AND ACTING: Create one of the following scenes that could be added to the play. You could devise the scene in groups, then write it down, or just write it by yourself.
(a)   The scene where Alcestis returns from the dead and is re-united with Admetus.
(b)   The scene where Persephone rejects Alcestis's death and returns her to life.

It may be that you could find a way of putting these two scenes together as one. For example, when Alcestis returns to Admetus, she tells him what happened to her in the land of the dead. As she begins to tell him, we see the scene played out in flashback.

ARTWORK: Design and draw a poster advertising the play. Think about what image you would choose to represent the play.

READING AND WRITING: Read the 'Background to the play'. Are there any other episodes in the lives of Admetus and Alcestis that you think might be turned into a short play, story or poem? You could choose one episode, and write something around it. Before you do, you'll probably have to find out more about that episode. Look in a book on Greek mythology such as *The Greek Myths: complete edition* by Robert Graves (Penguin paperback). You could also use the internet. One of the best websites I've come across is: Greek Mythology Link. The address is: http://hsa.brown.edu/~maicar/

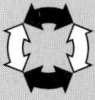 **READING AND DISCUSSION:** The Greek playright Euripides wrote a play based on the same story in 438BC. Here's an extract. It takes place a short time before Alcestis dies in her husband's place. Admetus has brought her out into the courtyard of the palace to see the sun for the last time.

ALCESTIS	Sun, and light of day, O turning wheel of the sky, clouds that fly.
ADMETUS	The sun sees you and me, two people suffering, who never hurt the gods so they should make you die.
ALCESTIS	My land, and palace arching my land, and marriage chambers of Iolcus, my own country.
ADMETUS	Raise yourself, my Alcestis, do not leave me now. I implore the gods to pity you. They have the power.
ALCESTIS	I see him there at the oars of his little boat in the lake, the ferryman of the dead, Charon, with his hand upon the oar, and he calls me now: 'What keeps you? Hurry, you hold us back.' He is urging me on in angry impatience.
ADMETUS	The crossing you speak of is a bitter one for me, ill starred; it is unfair we should be treated so.
ALCESTIS	Somebody has me, somebody takes me away, do you see, don't you see, to the courts of dead men. He frowns from under dark brows. He has wings. It is Death. Let me go, what are you doing, let go. Such is the road most wretched I have to walk.
ADMETUS	Sorrow for all who love you, most of all for me and for the children. All of us share in this grief.
ALCESTIS	Let me go now, let me down, flat. I have no strength to stand. Death is close to me. The darkness creeps over my eyes. O children, my children, you have no mother now, not any longer. Daylight is yours, my children. Look on it and be happy.

(Translated by Richard Lattimore in *The Greek Tragedies, Volume 3*, University of Chicago Press.)

Apart from bring written in verse, what other differences do you notice between the way the characters are presented in this extract, and the way they're presented in *Dead Man*?

Dramascripts

Queen of Hearts

Dramatised by
DAVID CALCUTT

BACKGROUND TO THE PLAY

Some three to four thousand years ago a great war between two branches of a noble family was fought in northern India. This war became the subject of many tales and stories which were told and re-told by travelling storytellers and bards over the ensuing centuries. Like all such tales and stories, it grew with the telling. And it became so popular that it began to attract other stories to it – in much the same way as did the legend of King Arthur – so that what began as the story of a war became a vast epic of the whole mythical life of India itself. The 'Mahabarata' as it has come to be known, was finally written down around eight hundred years ago, and it is now the longest written epic in the world, running to over ninety thousand verse couplets. It is seven times as long as the 'Iliad' and the 'Odyssey' of Homer put together. And it is still enormously popular in India today, although most people still come across it – or parts of it – in its oral rather than its written form.

In the epic, whatever real war may have given rise to the legend has been replaced by a mythical conflict involving heroes, heroines, demons, spirits, and gods. And radiating out from this central story are many other subsidiary stories, each self-contained, but also linking back to the central story, and to each other. The story of Savitri, on which *Queen of Hearts* is based, is one of these stories.

THE CHARACTERS

(in order of appearance)

1ST NARRATOR *(also* **ASHWAPATI** *King of Madra.)*

2ND NARRATOR *(also* **NARADA** *a wise man.)*

3RD NARRATOR *(also* **SAVITRI** *daughter of Ashwapati.)*

4TH NARRATOR *(also* **DYUMATSENA** *an exiled king.)*

5TH NARRATOR *(also* **SATYAVAN** *son of Dyumatsena.)*

DEATH

PRONOUNCING THE NAMES

ASHWAPATI *Ash-va-pati*

NARADA *Na-r-ad*

SAVITRI *Sa-vi-tree*

DYUMATSENA *Due-mat-sena*

SATYAVAN *Sat-ya-vahn*

QUEEN OF HEARTS

D EATH *is sitting on stage, shuffling a pack of cards. The other actors enter and speak as narrators.*

1ST NARRATOR	This is Death.	1
2ND NARRATOR	Death, sitting on this rock.	
3RD NARRATOR	Sitting on this rock, out in the middle of nowhere.	
4TH NARRATOR	Death, passing his time, playing a game of cards.	
5TH NARRATOR	A game he never loses.	

(DEATH stops shuffling the cards, takes one off the top, and turns it over. He holds it up and shows it to the NARRATORS.)

DEATH Ace of Spades.

(Puts the card back, and shuffles the pack again, as the NARRATORS speak.) 10

1ST NARRATOR Always the same.

(DEATH turns over a card.)

DEATH Ace of Spades.

2ND NARRATOR Turning up the same card.

(DEATH turns over a card.)

DEATH Ace of Spades.

3RD NARRATOR A winning hand.

(DEATH turns over a card.)

DEATH   Ace of Spades.

4TH NARRATOR   Never been known to fail.   2(

(DEATH turns over a card.)

DEATH   Ace of Spades.

5TH NARRATOR   Except once.

(DEATH looks up sharply at 5TH NARRATOR.)

DEATH   Impossible! I never lose! I'm Death! Surely, you know, Death
                       always wins.

                       *(DEATH turns over a card, looks at it with consternation, looks
                       at the NARRATORS, looks back to the card.)*

                       Queen of Hearts!

                       (Angrily, DEATH puts the card back into the pack, stands, and   3(
                       *goes to the side of the stage, where he sits, and shuffles the cards
                       again. The NARRATORS speak to the audience.)*

1ST NARRATOR   There was one occasion when Death didn't win.

2ND NARRATOR   A time when Death himself was outwitted.

3RD NARRATOR   Overcome by a power even stronger than his.

4TH NARRATOR   The power that moves the sun and all the stars!

5TH NARRATOR   And it happened like this.

2ND NARRATOR   There was a king, and his name was –

                       (1ST NARRATOR takes on the role of ASHWAPATI.)

ASHWAPATI   Ashwapati. A wealthy, powerful, and benevolent monarch.   40

 **with consternation** *With some alarm or shock.*

benevolent *Kind, charitable.*

2ND NARRATOR	And this king had a daughter. And her name was –
ASHWAPATI	Savitri.
	(3RD NARRATOR takes on the role of SAVITRI. She takes up a book, and reads. ASHWAPATI gazes on her, lovingly.)
4TH NARRATOR	Savitri was beautiful and generous –
5TH NARRATOR	Gentle and kind-hearted.
ASHWAPATI	All, in fact, that a daughter should be.
2ND NARRATOR	Or nearly all. She had one weakness. She was given to studying.
ASHWAPATI	Which is all very well. I'm a liberal-minded man. I believe that a woman should be educated. A keen mind is a great addition to her other, more traditional feminine qualities. *(He looks sharply at SAVITRI now.)* But it should be an enhancement, not a detraction! And in your case, my dear, I'm afraid your fondness for study is proving to be the latter.
4TH NARRATOR	What he meant was, there was no man who wanted to marry her.
ASHWAPATI	*(To SAVITRI.)* You're eighteen years old and you don't have a single suitor. And do you know why? You scare them! They're afraid you'll know more than they do!
SAVITRI	*(Not looking up from her book.)* I **do** know more than they do.
ASHWAPATI	You see? That's the kind of talk that keeps them away. If I didn't know you better, I'd say you were arrogant.
SAVITRI	*(Still not looking up from her book.)* You know I'm not arrogant, Father. I just speak the simple truth.

50

60

 **liberal-minded** *He means he's fairly open in his thinking.*

ASHWAPATI	That may be. But doesn't it worry you that men are scared of you? Don't you want a husband?
SAVITRI	*(Still not looking up.)* If he's the kind of husband who's afraid of learning – no, I don't.

70

ASHWAPATI	Then you'll have no husband at all! You'll remain unmarried!
SAVITRI	*(Still not looking up.)* Quite possibly.
ASHWAPATI	Savitri. Please listen to me. I'm your father, and I love you very much. I've always wanted the best for you. And I've always made sure you've had the best, haven't I?
SAVITRI	*(Still reading her book.)* Yes.
ASHWAPATI	When you were a little girl, the best toys. When you grew older, the best clothes. And the best books. You can't deny that, can you?

80

SAVITRI	*(Still reading her book.)* No, Father. You've been very good to me.
ASHWAPATI	I'm glad you think so. And now that you're grown up, my dear Savitri, now that you're a woman, I still want the best for you. I want you to have a husband. The best husband. Won't you at least consider it?
	(SAVITRI closes her book.)
SAVITRI	I have considered it, and I've come to a decision.
ASHWAPATI	At last.
SAVITRI	I want to travel.

90

ASHWAPATI	Travel? What do you mean? Travel where?
SAVITRI	Across the country. You were right about the books, Father. They are the very best. I've learned all I can from them, but I feel there's still more to learn . . .
ASHWAPATI	More!

SAVITRI   So I want to go on a journey to find the holiest and most
learned men in the land. I want to hear what they say and
learn from them. When I feel I've learned all a human
being can learn, I'll return. And then, if destiny wills it, I
shall find a husband.   **100**

ASHWAPATI   You're leaving it to destiny?

SAVITRI   In this book it says that all that happens to us is pre-
ordained. Our whole life is mapped out at our birth. If
that's the case, and if I am to marry, the man who will be
my husband exists somewhere, and the road I take shall
lead me to him.

(She gives the book to ASHWAPATI.)

Goodbye, Father. For the time being.

(SAVITRI turns from ASHWAPATI.)

5TH NARRATOR   And so Savitri left her home . . .   **110**

ASHWAPATI   And her father . . .

5TH NARRATOR   . . . and set off to find wisdom and understanding.

2ND NARRATOR   For a long time she searched, in many places . . .

4TH NARRATOR   . . . leaving her own country far behind . . .

2ND NARRATOR   . . . crossing hills and rivers . . .

4TH NARRATOR   . . . mountains and deserts . . .

5TH NARRATOR   . . . sleeping sometimes in a hut in a village . . .

2ND NARRATOR   . . . sometimes by the roadside, beneath the stars . . .

4TH NARRATOR   . . . she saw many wonders, she heard many strange tales . . .

   **all that happens to us is pre-ordained** *All that happens to us is
decided before we're born.*

5TH NARRATOR   . . . but wisdom always lay beyond, always just out of   120
reach . . .

(SAVITRI takes up the narration, looking around her as if seeing what she describes.)

SAVITRI   . . . until at last she came to a cave on the slopes of a high mountain. A wild place, it was, far from any human dwelling, overgrown with bushes and brambles, with a stream tumbling down through the rocks into a pool. A quiet, lonely place. And there, sitting at the mouth of the cave, looking directly at her, as if waiting for her . . .

*(2ND NARRATOR takes on the role of NARADA and turns to   130
face SAVITRI.)*

NARADA   A man.

4TH NARRATOR   Narada, the holy man.

5TH NARRATOR   The wise man.

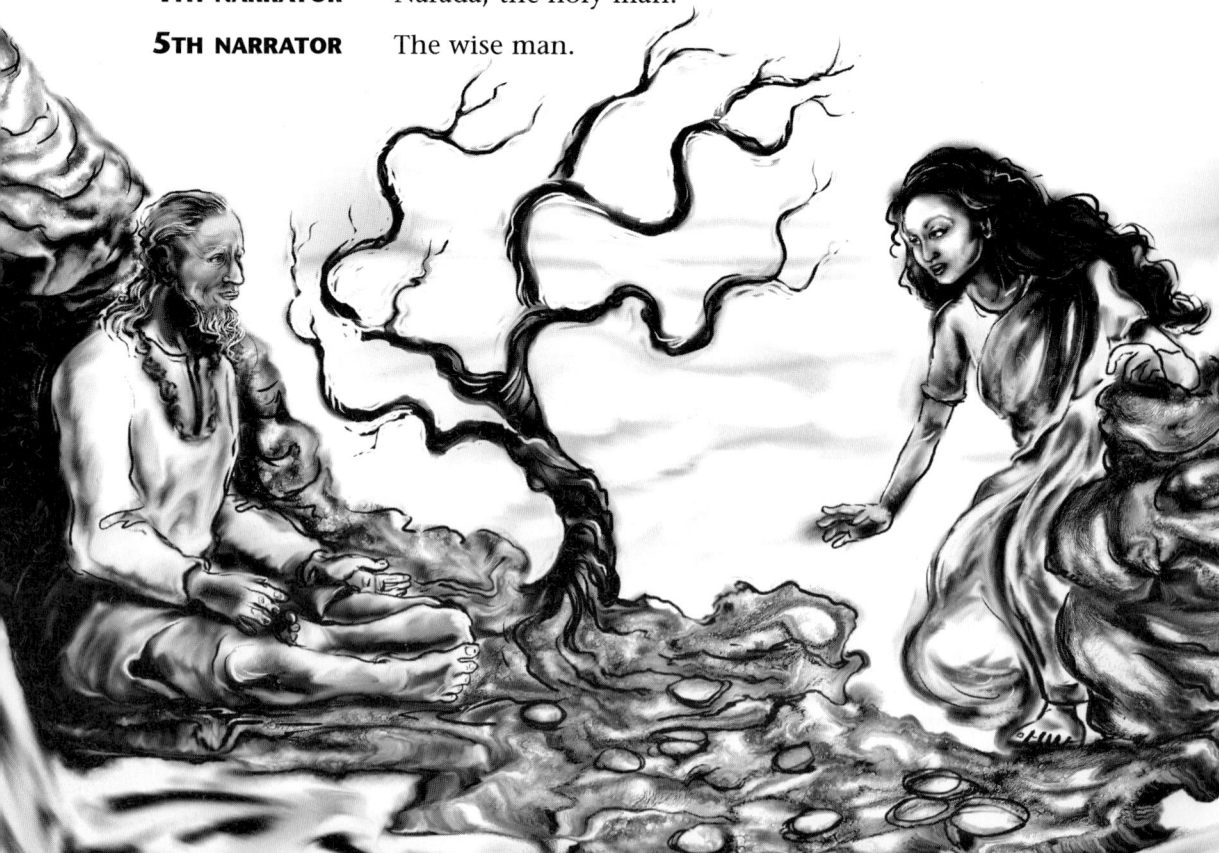

4TH NARRATOR	The Seer.
NARADA	I came here when I was a young man, to escape the noise and bustle of the world. I wanted peace. I wanted solitude. I wanted . . . to think. I've been here now a long time. I eat the berries and fruit that grow on the trees. I drink the water that falls into that pool. And I think. I contemplate. **140** And, through thinking and contemplation, through stillness and silence, I have, after so many years, attained some kind of . . . wisdom.

(SAVITRI speaks to NARADA.)

SAVITRI	I wish to share some of that wisdom. I wish to learn something of what you have learned. I wish you to be my teacher.
NARADA	Do you wish to learn for your own understanding, or for gain?
SAVITRI	For my own understanding. **150**
NARADA	How much do you wish to learn?
SAVITRI	All that can be taught.
NARADA	What do you know already?
SAVITRI	Nothing.
NARADA	Good. Let's sit here, outside the cave, and talk.

(SAVITRI and NARADA sit facing each other, as others narrate. ASHWAPATI speaks as NARRATOR.)

ASHWAPATI	So they sat and they talked.

The Seer *Literally, one who 'sees' things. Not, however, with the ordinary eye, but with the secret, 'inner' eye, the eye that can see into the future, or into the secret heart of things.*

contemplation *The calm, thoughtful study of something, as in meditation.*

4TH NARRATOR	They talked about many things.
5TH NARRATOR	They talked about the world, and its creation. 160
ASHWAPATI	They talked about the world, and its destruction.
4TH NARRATOR	And how creation and destruction are both the same thing . . .
5TH NARRATOR	And the end of one world is the beginning of another . . .
ASHWAPATI	And the beginning of one world is the end of another.
4TH NARRATOR	Then they talked about how to live in the world . . .
5TH NARRATOR	The best way of living, and the worst way of living . . .
ASHWAPATI	How thought should always come before speech . . .
4TH NARRATOR	How stillness should always come before action . . .
5TH NARRATOR	And how good speech and good deeds are the keys to right 170 living.
ASHWAPATI	So they talked, and time passed.
4TH NARRATOR	They ate the fruits and the berries that grew on the trees . . .
5TH NARRATOR	They drank the water that ran into the pool.
ASHWAPATI	And the days passed and the nights passed . . .
4TH NARRATOR	A whole year passed . . .
5TH NARRATOR	And at the end of that year, Narada said . . .
NARADA	There's no more I can teach you, now. You've learned all you can. Besides, I'm tired, and I want to be alone again. Whatever else there is to be known, and understood, you 180 must find out for yourself. It's time for you to go back into the world.
	(SAVITRI narrates and enacts what she narrates.)
SAVITRI	Then Savitri stood, and thanked the holy man for his time, and said goodbye to him, and turned to go. But as she was leaving, he called her back.

NARADA	One thing, before you go. You've been a good pupil. I'd like to give you something to take with you.
SAVITRI	Please, you needn't . . .
NARADA	What I give you is a warning. A prediction. You told me your father wished you to marry.

190

SAVITRI	Yes, that's true.
NARADA	But that there was no man you wished to marry yourself.
SAVITRI	If he lives, I haven't met him yet.
NARADA	He lives. And you will meet him. That's my prediction. Now here's my warning. The man you meet, the man whom you will wish to marry, has a curse upon him. The curse of death.
SAVITRI	All men and women live under that curse.
NARADA	It's true, we all know that we're going to die. But the time of our death is unknown. That's why we go on living. But this man's time is fixed. A year after you meet him, he will die. A year to the very day. There. That's my gift. Do with it as you see fit.

200

(NARADA turns from SAVITRI.)

ASHWAPATI	So it happened that as Savitri was returning home . . .
4TH NARRATOR	Along a path that led through a forest . . .
5TH NARRATOR	And as it was drawing towards evening . . .
ASHWAPATI	And she was tired because she'd been walking all day . . .
4TH NARRATOR	She sat to rest beneath a tree . . .

210

5TH NARRATOR	And as she sat there, she sang.

(SAVITRI narrates.)

SAVITRI	It was a song from her childhood, a sweet and simple song. She sang it softly at first, but then she let her voice rise,

because that song, and the singing of it, reminded her of home, and all that she loved best in the world.

(4TH NARRATOR takes on the role of DYUMATSENA, a blind man.)

ASHWAPATI And as she was singing, an old man came walking out of the trees. He stood by the path, his eyes wide and staring, 220 silent, listening to Savitri's song.

5TH NARRATOR But when Savitri saw him, she stopped.

DYUMATSENA Please! Don't stop singing. It's been a long time since I heard anything so beautiful as your voice.

(SAVITRI narrates.)

SAVITRI But she didn't carry on singing. The old man's sudden appearance had surprised her too much – and frightened her a little, too. She just sat there, silent, beneath the tree.

DYUMATSENA Why have you become silent? Are you still there? Or have you gone. Perhaps you were a spirit, and I've scared you 230 away. Or perhaps . . . perhaps you were only my dream . . .

ASHWAPATI And it was then that Savitri realised that the old man couldn't see her. He was blind.

NARADA So she stood, and spoke gently to him.

(SAVITRI speaks to DYUMATSENA.)

SAVITRI I haven't gone away. I'm still here. And I'm not a spirit or a dream. I'm an ordinary girl. I'm making my way home. My name's Savitri.

DYUMATSENA Savitri. Your voice is as beautiful when you speak as when you sing. My name is Dyumatsena. I suppose I must have 240 startled you.

SAVITRI Yes, you did, a little. I didn't expect to come upon anyone in this forest.

DYUMATSENA I live here with my son. We have a hut not far from here.

	You say you're making your way home. Is it far?	
SAVITRI	I have many days to travel yet.	
DYUMATSENA	It's growing late. You won't reach the end of the forest before nightfall. And it's not good to be alone here after dark. Come with me to our hut. We'll give you something to eat and drink, and you can rest there for the night.	250
SAVITRI	Thank you. You're very generous.	
DYUMATSENA	Not completely. I have a selfish motive. I want to hear you sing again.	
SAVITRI	And you shall.	
DYUMATSENA	Follow me. Although I'm blind, my feet can find their way.	
	(SAVITRI and DYUMATSENA cross to another part of the stage, where 5TH NARRATOR takes on the role of SATYAVAN, as others narrate.)	
ASHWAPATI	She followed the blind man a short way through the forest, until they came to a small clearing . . .	260
NARADA	. . . where there was a hut, and a fire burning outside it, and a young man cooking food over the fire.	
DYUMATSENA	This is my son, Satyavan. Satyavan, this is Savitri.	
	(SATYAVAN narrates.)	
SATYAVAN	Satyavan greeted Savitri. He asked her to sit by the fire.	
SAVITRI	Savitri sat by the fire.	
DYUMATSENA	And Satyavan's father sat as well.	
	(All three are sitting now.)	
ASHWAPATI	Then Satyavan shared out the food he'd been cooking.	
NARADA	Simple food – but well-cooked, and welcome.	270
ASHWAPATI	And after they'd eaten and drunk their fill, Satyavan's father asked Savitri to sing.	

NARADA	Which she did.
SAVITRI	She sang the song she'd been singing in the forest, and her voice rose softly in the darkening air.
SATYAVAN	She sang as the night deepened, and firelight flickered on their faces.
DYUMATSENA	And to Dyumatsena, it was once more as if he were hearing the voice of a heavenly spirit, singing out of a dream.
SATYAVAN	And to Satyavan, it was the voice of his own love and longing, singing to him from the depth of his heart.
ASHWAPATI	At last she finished. Her voice died away. Only the silence of the night and the crackling of the dying flames remained.
NARADA	Then Dyumatsena stirred himself, and stood up, stiffly.
DYUMATSENA	I'm tired. I'm going in. Satyavan, make sure that Savitri has somewhere comfortable to sleep. Comfortable, and safe.
SATYAVAN	Of course, Father.
DYUMATSENA	*(To SAVITRI.)* Savitri. Your singing has brought back to me, for a little while, the tenderness and happiness of my former days. Days when the world was as sweet to me as your song. I thank you truly for it.
	(DYUMATSENA moves away from SAVITRI and SATYAVAN as others narrate.)
ASHWAPATI	But Savitri and Satyavan remained sitting together, in the dark, by the firelight.
NARADA	And she told him who she was, of her father, and her father's kingdom . . .
ASHWAPATI	And of her journey to find wisdom, and her year of learning with Narada, the holy man.
NARADA	Then, when she'd finished, Satyavan sat in silence for a time. And then he told her his story.

280

290

300

(SATYAVAN speaks to SAVITRI.)

SATYAVAN My father, too, was once a king, though you wouldn't know it to see him now. He was a good king, benevolent to all his people. And all loved him. Except his brother, my uncle. He hated my father, and plotted to overthrow him. My father suspected nothing. He loved my uncle dearly, and never dreamed he would wish him any harm. One day my uncle burst into my father's room. With him was a force of **310** soldiers. He revealed to my father how much he hated him, told him he was overthrown, banished him from the kingdom. He, his brother, would rule in his place. And then my father wept. Not for his lost crown or his stolen kingdom. He wept because his heart was broken. And the tears he wept were so bitter they burned his eyes and he became blind. I was only a child then, hardly able to understand all that was happening. But I became my father's sole companion and guide. We wandered the roads and villages as beggars, and often kind people took pity on **320** us, gave us something to eat, a bed for the night. But what my father now truly desired was to live in solitude. So at last we came here, to this forest. I built this hut for us. We've lived here since then. And though he's not found happiness, there are times when his heart is lighter, and moments when his wounded spirit is at peace. And one of those times was now, tonight, when you sang.

(Characters narrate. During this narration, SAVITRI and SATYAVAN, in a very simple way, enact what is described.)

ASHWAPATI His story was finished. It was late. The fire was dying down. **330**

NARADA And as the night was warm and clear, he made up a bed of leaves for Savitri on one side of the fire . . .

DYUMATSENA . . . and a bed of leaves for himself on the other side of the fire . . .

ASHWAPATI And each lay there in the dark, watching the flickering of the dying flames . . .

NARADA	. . . and the flickering of the distant, dying stars . . .
DYUMATSENA	. . . and neither of them slept.
SAVITRI	Savitri's heart ached with pity for the story of what had happened to Satyavan and his father. But it wasn't only pity 340 that made it ache.
SATYAVAN	Satyavan's heart was filled with longing for the song Savitri had sung. But it wasn't only the song for which his heart longed.
ASHWAPATI	And at last, when the night was over, and the light of morning touched the sky . . .
NARADA	As Satyavan rose, and blew on the embers of the fire, and as the flames began to flicker again . . .
DYUMATSENA	And as Savitri helped him to collect wood for the fire, and as they built the fire up again . . . 350
SATYAVAN	Each knew for certain what their hearts had spoken.
SAVITRI	Each knew that they loved the other.
	(SAVITRI and SATYAVAN are now standing facing each other. SATYAVAN's father, DYUMATSENA, approaches them.)
DYUMATSENA	Of course you will have my consent, and my blessing – my most deep and heartfelt blessing. But your father, Savitri? What will he say to his daughter marrying the son of a poor, blind man? Will he give his consent?
SAVITRI	My father loves me, as I love him. His only desire is my happiness. And my happiness is to marry your son, to be 360 the wife of Satyavan. My father will give his consent and his blessing.
DYUMATSENA	And you, Savitri. Will you be content to live here, in a poor hut in the forest? You are a king's daughter.
SAVITRI	Satyavan is a king's son. One of the things I learned from the holy man, Narada, is that outward things of the world

are as nothing compared to those of the inner world – the world of the spirit and the heart. That's where our true home lies. Hut or palace, forest or rich kingdom, all are one, if the heart's content. 370

DYUMATSENA (*To SATYAVAN.*) My son, you're to be blessed with a wise wife as well as a loving one. No man can ask for more.

SATYAVAN I know that, Father. I think there's much that I can learn from her.

DYUMATSENA Much indeed. But now we must celebrate. Satyavan, take your bow. Go into the forest and find us something good to eat. Something fit for a betrothal feast. And after we've feasted, you must go with Savitri to meet her father, and obtain his blessing.

SATYAVAN Very well, Father. 380

(*SATYAVAN turns, and moves away. NARADA narrates.*)

NARADA Satyavan took his bow and went into the forest. And as soon as he was gone, the old man turned to Savitri – and Savitri could see what he'd been hiding all this time – a terrible sadness that rose up from his heart, and fell in tears from his blind eyes.

SAVITRI (*To DYUMATSENA.*) Why are you crying? Tell me what your sadness is.

DYUMATSENA I'm crying for the first time since I was cast out from my kingdom. Then, I wept because I had lost a brother. Now I 390 weep, because I know I shall lose a son.

SAVITRI How will you lose him?

betrothal feast *When a couple become engaged to be married they are 'betrothed' – promised to each other. This 'betrothal' can be marked by a feast or celebration of some kind.*

DYUMATSENA	What I'm about to tell you, Satyavan does not know. Only I know it. I've kept it from him. When you learn what it is, you'll understand why. I'd thought to keep it from you as well. But I can't. It's only fair that you know.
SAVITRI	Know what?
DYUMATSENA	That my son is going to die. He was born cursed. A holy man told me that on the day my son met the woman he wished to marry – on the very day that he found love – 400 within a year of that day, death would take him.

(There is a pause.)

You're silent. You say nothing. Perhaps you're deciding you can no longer marry my son. I won't blame you. Once my son is dead, as his widow, you can never marry again.

SAVITRI	Do you think that I would wish to marry anyone again? I love Satyavan. I shall never love anyone else.
DYUMATSENA	Even so – you may wish to save yourself the pain of seeing your husband die.
SAVITRI	Listen, what you've told me, I already knew. Narada told me 410 that the only man I would ever love was doomed to die a year after I met him. When I knew I loved your son, I also knew I had a choice – to say nothing and to leave here, return to my father, and never marry. Or to speak, take Satyavan as my husband, and accept his fate as mine. I made my choice. I didn't think twice about it. And I shall never regret the choice that I made.

(SAVITRI turns from DYUMATSENA. Characters narrate now.)

NARADA	After they'd celebrated their betrothal, Savitri and Satyavan left the forest. 420
SATYAVAN	They went to Savitri's home, to see her father, and obtain his blessing.
ASHWAPATI	And though he could not understand his daughter's wish to

marry this man – when she could marry any man she wanted . . .

SAVITRI He respected her wish, and gave them his blessing.

NARADA And they returned to the forest, to begin their life together.

DYUMATSENA A doomed life, though Satyavan did not know it. A life where every day was precious.

SAVITRI Every moment of every day. 430

NARADA And those days and those moments passed swiftly, as all things of the earth must pass . . .

ASHWAPATI Until, at last, the sun rose on the day . . .

DEATH . . . when Death came walking in the forest.

(DEATH rises and slowly approaches SATYAVAN, as SATYAVAN and SAVITRI narrate.)

SATYAVAN A warm day, it was, the sky a deep blue above the trees, the sun's rays golden as they fell through the leaves.

SAVITRI They were walking home through the forest, Savitri carrying a basket of fruit, Satyavan the wood that he had cut. 440

SATYAVAN They were thirsty, and they stopped to drink at a pool.

SAVITRI Savitri drank first. She knelt beside the pool, and scooped the clear, cold water up with her hands. Then she sat on the grass, as Satyavan knelt to drink.

SATYAVAN He knelt, and leaned forward over the pool. He saw his own face reflected in the water. He raised his hands to scoop up the water. And then he stopped. For there, in the water beside his own, another face was reflected.

(DEATH is now standing above and behind the kneeling SATYAVAN.) 450

DEATH Death's face. It was Death's face he saw. And at the moment of seeing it, his life ended. The world became a place of

	shadows. He forgot his father. He forgot Savitri. He forgot himself.
SATYAVAN	He felt nothing. He saw nothing. He heard nothing. Only Death's voice. All he heard was Death's voice speaking to him.
	(DEATH speaks to SATYAVAN.)
DEATH	Rise. Look at me.
	(SATYAVAN stands. He turns and faces DEATH.) 460
	I am Death. You have seen my face. From now on it is all you will ever see. Leave this place now, and come with me.
	(SAVITRI cries out.)
SAVITRI	No!
	(DEATH turns, surprised, to SAVITRI.)
	No, you will not take him.
DEATH	You see me?
SAVITRI	Yes, I see you, and I know who you are. You are Yama, the god of death.
DEATH	Then you know why I am here. 470
SAVITRI	I know. For a long time I've waited for this day, and I did not know what I would do when it arrived. But now I know that I will not let you take my husband.
DEATH	He is no longer your husband. The man your husband was is gone. From this moment he is mine. He must go with me.
SAVITRI	Then he will not go alone.
DEATH	What? You'll come with us?
SAVITRI	Yes. I swore never to leave him, and I never shall.
DEATH	It's a long journey. 480

SAVITRI	I'm prepared to make it. I shall not leave him.
DEATH	Come with us, then, if you wish. But it's a barren journey you'll make. And one you'll return from alone.
	(DEATH, SAVITRI and SATYAVAN face the audience as others narrate.)
ASHWAPATI	Death turned and led Satyavan away through the forest. And Savitri followed.
NARADA	Deeper into the forest they went, along a path no human had trodden before . . .
ASHWAPATI	And no bird sang, and no creature moved, no wind stirred the leaves on the trees . . .
NARADA	And Savitri was scratched by thorn and briars, her clothes were torn by branches and twigs . . .
ASHWAPATI	She stumbled, she twisted her feet on thick roots, but still she followed.
NARADA	Until they came to the edge of that forest, and Death stopped, and turned to her and said . . .
DEATH	From here, the road grows even more difficult. You have proved how deep your love is. Go back, now, and I'll give you a gift to take with you. You may ask me for anything you wish – except the life of your husband.
SAVITRI	I'll ask you for this – let my father-in-law's sight be returned to him. Let him be blind no more.
DEATH	I grant you that wish. It's done.
ASHWAPATI	And as Death spoke . . .
NARADA	Upon that instant . . .
DYUMATSENA	Satyavan's father could see again! He saw the trees, he saw the leaves that grew on the trees. He saw the sunlight shining through those leaves, and the blue sky above, and the grass below. He saw the world, and all the colours of the world. And he saw too that he was alone.

490

500

510

(DEATH speaks to SAVITRI.)

DEATH   Now leave us. We must go on.

SAVITRI   If you must go on, then so must I. I will not leave my husband.

(Others narrate again.)

ASHWAPATI   Now they walked through a barren land. Cliffs towered high above them . . .

NARADA   And the road they trod was rocky and jagged, and Savitri's feet were bloody and torn . . .   520

ASHWAPATI   But still she went on, because her pain and suffering meant nothing to her, still she went on along that road . . .

NARADA   Which led to the foot of a high mountain, and there Death stopped and spoke once more.

(DEATH speaks to SAVITRI.)

DEATH   Your courage and fortitude have earned my deepest respect and admiration. But now, as you can see, we must climb this mountain. You surely cannot follow us there. Before we part, however, I'll make a second gift to you. Once more you may ask for anything you wish – except, as I said   530 before, the life of your husband.

SAVITRI   This is my second wish. And again, it is nothing for myself. Let my father-in-law's crown and kingdom be returned to him.

DEATH   As you wish. They are returned.

ASHWAPATI   And upon that instant . . .

NARADA   As Death's words were spoken . . .

DYUMATSENA   . . . Satyavan's father was king once more. All that had happened in the past was erased, all was as if it had never been. He was in his palace. He was wearing his fine robes.   540 The crown of kingship was on his head. His servants stood by him, his nobles and courtiers. Music played. Women danced. But his son was not there.

DEATH   Now, I will say goodbye to you. Take your road, and I shall take mine.

SAVITRI   The road you take and the road I take are one and the same. I have told you before, I will not leave my husband.

(Others narrate.)

ASHWAPATI   Now they began to climb the mountain.

NARADA   Hard going, over the treacherous peaks . . .   550

ASHWAPATI   And the black crags where the wind wailed.

NARADA   Higher they climbed, through mist and clouds . . .

ASHWAPATI   The air growing thin, the ice burning . . .

NARADA   Till suddenly the earth fell away . . .

ASHWAPATI   And they stood at the utmost end of the world . . .

NARADA   Where the tip of the mountain touched the sky's top.

(DEATH speaks to SAVITRI.)

DEATH Who would have thought you would follow Death to the earth's edge? No living mortal has ever come this far. Look down there. Look down the other side of the mountain, and tell me what you see. 560

SAVITRI I see . . . shadow. The whole land shrouded in shadow that swirls like a black fog. And nothing more. Nothing beneath that or beyond that. From here outwards, in all directions, to the horizon, and beyond the horizon – a world of shadow.

DEATH What you see is my kingdom, the land of the dead. I must go there, now, and I must take with me the man who was once your husband. And you will not be able to follow us there. 570

SAVITRI I've followed you to the end of the world. I can follow beyond the end.

DEATH Don't deceive yourself. Did you learn nothing during the year you spent with the holy man? Human life must be lived within bounds and limits. They are necessary to maintain the balance of creation. If those limits are crossed, the balance is upset, and creation is plunged into chaos. Were you to attempt to place one foot within my kingdom, before your due time, the fabric of the world would be torn apart. Are you willing to risk that for the sake of this one 580 man?

balance of creation . . . fabric of the world *The thinking behind this speech is that all existence works like some complex piece of machinery – a clockwork watch, perhaps, with all the parts balanced to interact with each other. If one of these parts is damaged, the whole, finely tuned mechanism would stop working. Death, as the natural end of life, is one of the 'working parts' of creation. In attempting to win her husband back from the dead, Savitri is threatening to 'damage' this particular working part, and thus threatening the working of the whole of existence.*

ASHWAPATI	Savitri said nothing. She was silent.
NARADA	She knew that Death spoke the truth.
ASHWAPATI	She could not disrupt the nature of things.
NARADA	She could not plunge the world into chaos.
ASHWAPATI	And she knew that now she must return home, bearing her grief in her arms . . .
NARADA	Nurse it and nurture it, her only child.
DEATH	*(To SAVITRI.)* But I will give you something that will perhaps make that grief a little easier. A third time, you may 590 ask for anything – except the life of your husband.
ASHWAPATI	Savitri stood awhile in thought. She could think of nothing she wanted.
NARADA	All she wanted was here, and it was lost to her.
ASHWAPATI	And then that loss spoke to her.
NARADA	And there, at the world's end, above the place of shadow and death . . .
DYUMATSENA	. . . where there was no hope, hope came.
SAVITRI	You have given my father-in-law his sight. You have given him back his kingdom. Now, will you give him happiness? 600
DEATH	Yes, I will.
SAVITRI	You promise?
DEATH	Once I give my word, it will not be taken back.
SAVITRI	Then the one thing that will make my father-in-law truly happy is this – to see his grandchildren playing at his feet, and to see them grow to full health and happiness.
ASHWAPATI	And now Death was silent. He knew he had been outwitted.
NARADA	Because, as yet, Savitri had no children. And only with her husband could she have children.

ASHWAPATI	And he'd given his word and could not take it back.	610
NARADA	The promise he'd made would have to be kept.	
DEATH	Savitri. It's a brave and courageous woman who would follow Death to the edge of his own kingdom. And it's a wise woman who would dare to trick Death himself. You have looked on despair and found hope. You have gazed into Death's face and found life. So I give your husband back to you. Go, now, the two of you. Return to the world. Live there together, with your children. And live happily.	
	(DEATH turns and walks back to where he was sitting. All now speak as narrators.)	620
ASHWAPATI	And Death was gone.	
NARADA	The mountain was gone.	
DYUMATSENA	Savitri and Satyavan stood once more in the forest, by the pool where they had knelt to drink.	
SATYAVAN	Sunlight shone through the trees. Birds sang. Flowers bloomed among the grass. The whole earth felt warm, and fresh, and alive.	
SAVITRI	And Savitri took her husband's hand, and she smiled at him . . .	
SATYAVAN	. . . and he smiled at her . . .	630
SAVITRI	And together they walked back into their lives.	
ASHWAPATI	Lives that were fruitful.	
NARADA	Lives that were blessed.	
DYUMATSENA	Lives that were lived in contentment and happiness.	
DEATH	Until Death came to claim them, as he does all those who walk in the world.	
	(He shuffles the pack, turns a card over, looks at it, looks up, smiles and places the card down.)	
	Ace of Spades.	

ACTING: In the play, apart from Death, all the characters are also narrators. This means the actors have two roles to play – one as the character they are playing, and one as a storyteller. If you were producing the play for the stage, how would you make this clear to the audience? In small groups, choose a short section from the play where the actors move between being characters and narrators, and try performing it in different ways. If others do this, look at each others' work, and discuss which ways of performing the scene you think work best.

ACTING: There are two journey scenes in the play – Savitri's journey to find Narada, and her journey when she follows Death. These journeys are narrated. But, in performance, they could also be shown visually by the actors creating images with their bodies. In small groups, choose one of the two journeys and try and create them using still images. When you're satisfied with this, try adding the narration. Discuss how you think this works as a piece of theatre.

WRITING: The play is based on a folk-tale. Often – though not always – folk-tales tell us some simple truth about people, or the world, or they offer advice on how to live in the world. What do you think this story is telling us about ourselves? Or do you think it's meant simply as a piece of entertainment? See if you can write down, in a single short sentence or phrase, what you think the play is about. Then compare this with what others have written.

RESEARCH AND READING: There are many folk-tales dealing with Death. There's a story in which a soldier is given a magic bag in which he catches Death, so that no-one can ever die. And there's the Greek story of Orpheus who goes to Hades to try and bring back his dead wife, Eurydice. Find some books of myths and folk-tales from the library, and see how many stories about Death you can find. Read a few, and see what similarities they might have.

ARTWORK: Design and draw one of the following:
- a costume for one of the characters
- a simple set for the whole play, which can represent all locations
- a poster advertising the play.

FURTHER READING: *The Ramayana* is a great Indian epic which tells the story of Prince Rama and Princess Sita, and the war against the demon Ravana. It's a long story, originally written in verse, but there are several shorter, simplified versions in prose. You could look for a copy in your local bookshop or library, or look at a collection of Indian myths and folk-tales. (You can find a dramatised version in Dramascripts: *Local Heroes*.) There is an excellent Indian mythology website: bttp://indianmythology.com

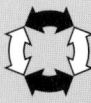 **WRITING A PLAY:** Below is a brief summary of another folk-tale from India. When you've read it, think about how you might turn this into a short play. You can either devise the play in small groups, or write it on your own. Here are some basic guidelines to follow:

- Decide which characters are going to be in the play.
- Work out a scenario for the play. A scenario is simply a list of the scenes, and what happens in each scene.
- Decide if you're going to use narrative (storytelling) in the play. If you are, who is going to do the narrating? A storyteller? One of the characters? Several or all of the characters? This will determine the way in which the play will be created.
- Find ways of moving easily from one scene to the next, or one location to the next, and of letting the audience know where each scene is taking place. It's best not to rely on the use of lighting for this, or a set.
- It should be possible to perform the finished play in any kind of space – a hall, or drama room, or classroom, and with the least amount of preparation. This means trying to use simple costumes and props.

Here's a summary of the story:

A Brahmin and his wife live in a small village. A Brahmin is a Hindu priest. They are both very poor, and face starvation. At his wife's suggestion, the Brahmin goes into the forest and prays to the goddess Durga to help them. Durga appears and, because the Brahmin has always been a devout priest, gives him a pot which will cook food whenever it's required. The Brahmin takes the pot home, and, for a while, he and his wife eat well and live happily. But the Head Man of the village hears about the pot and wants it for himself. It so happens that the Head Man's daughter is getting married, and he invites the Brahmin and his wife to be guests at her wedding. It's tradition that all guests bring a gift for the bride. But the Brahmin and his wife, being poor, have nothing to give – except the pot. The Head Man pretends to be outraged. To save themselves from being shamed in front of the whole village, the Brahmin and his wife give the pot to the Head Man's daughter. Later, of course, the Head Man takes the pot for himself.

Now they face starvation again. The Brahmin returns once more to the forest and prays to Durga to help him and his wife a second time. Durga appears again, and again gives the Brahmin a pot. But, when he gets the pot home, instead of it cooking food when asked, a terrible demon leaps out of the pot and beats the Brahmin with a club. But now his wife has an idea. Pretending that this second pot is even better than the first, she persuades the Head Man to give them back the first pot in exchange for the second. Eager to try out this second pot, the Head Man speaks the required words and the demon once more appears. It beats the Head Man with the club, chases him out of the village, and neither of them are seen again. With the first pot back in their care, the Brahmin and his wife see to it that neither they, nor anyone else in the village, ever go hungry again.

LOOKING BACK AT THE PLAYS

1 DISCUSSION

Discuss which of the three plays you liked best, and give reasons why you liked that particular play more than the others.

2 DISCUSSION AND WRITING: A REVIEW

Use ideas from the above discussion to write a review of the play you liked best. Compare it with the other two.

3 WRITING

Note down all the things the three plays have in common – themes, subject matter, style of writing, and so on. Use these notes to write about the similarity between the three plays.

4 DISCUSSION

Discuss why you think I chose the title 'Love and Loss' for the three plays. Do you think it's a good title? Can you think of another?

5 WRITING

Write your own poems or stories that deal with the theme of Death.

6 ARTWORK

Design a poster for a production of *Love and Loss*. The design should make reference to all three plays.

7 WRITING

Many myths and religions have stories about how Death came into the world. They tell of a time when people lived in idyllic circumstances, and did not die. Then, through some mistake or folly, they brought Death upon themselves. The myth of Adam and Eve is one such story.

Another, from South America, tells how a young man is brought up by an old woman. She sends him into the world to help people out, and he becomes a great hero – he frees them from drought, brings them fire, and so on. Eventually, a sickness comes to the people and he's unable to cure them. So he calls on his mother to help him. His mother crosses the river into the world, and cures people of the sickness by taking their lives. She is, in fact, Death, and has been waiting for someone to call her into the world. Now she's in it, and can never leave it. The young man is cursed by people and becomes an outcast – the only human being who still lives for ever.

Try making up and writing your own myth about how Death came into the world.

8   ARTWORK

Choose one play and make a storyboard of the main episodes, in order. Add captions to each picture to explain what is going on.

9   COSTUME DESIGN

The stories on which these plays are based existed long before they were written down. There is therefore no particular time when the stories take place. If you were designing the costumes for a production of one of these plays, in what period of time would you have it set? What kinds of clothes would the characters wear? You could decide to have different times and periods represented in the costumes. And you could costume the characters according to their personalities. Try sketching designs for two or three of the characters and write a short piece for each one saying why you have come to your decision.